# THE ARCHITECTURE OF
# Kallmann McKinnell & Wood

BY DAVID DILLON

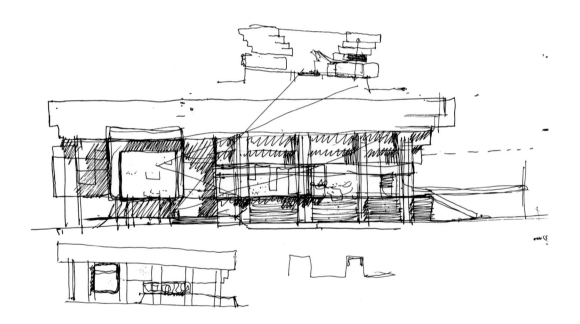

First published in
the United States of America
by Edizioni Press, Inc.
469 West 21st Street
New York, New York 10011
www.edizionipress.com
ISBN: 1-931536-31-7
Library of Congress Catalog Card Number: 2004113201

Printed in China

Editor: Aaron Seward
Cover photo: Steve Rosenthal
Back cover photo: Robert Benson

# Introduction

BY DAVID DILLON

1

In a lecture honoring the late Pietro Belluschi, Michael McKinnell described his own firm's work as a blend of memory and invention. "We believe neither in the iconoclastic gesture nor in conformity," he explained, staking out the modernist middle ground where the honoree himself once stood. "Both acknowledge tradition but both are simplistic concepts." Simplistic because one acknowledges tradition by undermining it, the other by slavishly copying it. Either path leads to shallow, convictionless architecture in which idea easily devolves into polemic or pastiche. The architecture of Kallmann McKinnell & Wood doesn't depend on exotic forms or glib mimesis. They neither build theory nor chase fashion. They have instead developed a sophisticated, if unclassifiable, synthesis of old and new, traditional and contemporary, familiar and surprising. Although critics have occasionally pinned the postmodern label on them, it hasn't stuck. Their work is circumstantial rather than narrowly ideological, expressing no particular bias about how the world should look or run. Its constancies and continuities—the articulated plane, the eloquent fragment, the slyly subversive wit mixed with conspicuous gravitas—have not hardened into a house style that can be applied like Drivit to whatever commission comes along. They start from the assumption that every building is unique, with its own special place and needs, and that there are no all-purpose solutions. Such a delicate balance didn't just happen; it is the product of forty years of patient exploration and occasional reversals.

When Gerhard Kallmann and Michael McKinnell arrived on the scene in the late 1950s, they were committed—some would say evangelical—Brutalists. Their first projects—Boston City Hall (**1**), the Boston Five Cents Savings Bank, and the Love Gymnasium at Phillips Exeter Academy—were bold compositions of steel, stone, concrete, and glass that celebrated mass and raw abstract monumentality, and that made no allowances for small sensory pleasures that might appeal to the fictive general public. Instead of convention and emotional reassurance, they offered toughness and the allure of the primitive, as though shock were an appropriate complement to firmness, commodity, and delight. In a 1959 lecture, Kallmann dismissed "agreeable aesthetic effects" in favor of "a new architecture…expressive only of the process of [its] genesis. The buildings communicate only the manner of their own making, and do not declare themselves in terms other than those of architectural actuality." His essays from this period, published mainly in *Architectural Forum* and *Architectural Record*, also endorse the "frank expression of structure," and "disregard of human content, which is the essence of Brutalism." English émigré Michael McKinnell, his graduate assistant at Columbia University before becoming his partner, took an equally unsentimental view of modern architecture. "At that time I was totally consumed with formal and spatial issues," he recalls. "I believed that architecture must seek its roots in construction and I wasn't really interested in what the users of the building might think or want."

Kallmann, McKinnell & Knowles' victory in the 1962 Boston City Hall Competition was one of the most remarkable debuts in American architectural history. Three young architects, two of them foreigners without a building to their names, beat out half a dozen larger and more established firms with a design that was intricate and confrontational, but also powerfully evocative. "A reservoir of themes for our later work," Kallmann later called it.

Yet a celebrated first building, like a celebrated first novel or first film, can be a coup or a curse. For Kallmann McKinnell & Wood (Henry Wood joined the firm when Edward Knowles decided to remain in New York City), it was a bit of both, projecting them onto the covers of the international design magazines but also typecasting them. In the years immediately after their triumph, KMW received widespread critical acclaim but few commissions. "Prospective clients thought either that we only designed monuments, or because we were only four or five people we couldn't possibly handle a really big job," says McKinnell. " 'Just give us a chance,' we kept pleading, but nobody would."

2

KMW supported themselves and the office with small projects—a park, a neighborhood library—and by teaching at Harvard's Graduate School of Design, from which many of their best designers have come. Their big break came in 1977, when the American Academy of Arts and Sciences commissioned the firm to design its new house in Cambridge. And house is the operative word. The Academy, an exclusive group sprinkled with Nobel laureates, wasn't interested in another Brutalist monument; its program, in fact, explicitly forbade the use of exposed concrete. It was looking instead for the kinds of sensory richness and "agreeable esthetic effects" that the partners had previously spurned, along with the genteel amplitude of a turn-of-the-century country house and a dash of the English picturesque in the landscaping. Elements of previous work, such as a commanding central atrium and suites of interlocking rooms, reappear but in more intimate, domestic form. "In a magical garden reminiscent of a painting by Poussin," the architects later wrote, "we were permitted to build an ideal villa, where magisterial games of the mind could be played and given architectural form." (2)

Working on the Academy made KMW more responsive to issues of intimacy and ordinary human comfort, and to embrace an urbanism that was more contextual than confrontational. The shift was partly pragmatic—Brutalism was dead and they had no work—and partly circumstantial. Robert Venturi's *Complexity and Contradiction in Architecture* (1966) had caused a seismic shift within the profession, away from pure architectural solutions and toward history, pattern, and a new inclusiveness that allowed for the dumb and the ordinary as well as the grand and the cerebral. Despite his enthusiasm for shock effects, Gerhard Kallmann and his partners were quietly receptive to Venturi's exhortations. In a 1958 essay, he had described Torre Velasca, Belgiojoso, and Rogers' controversial medievalized apartment/office tower in Milan (3), as a "valiant essay in the neglected art of fitting modern architecture into a historic continuity of building." And while he occasionally faulted the architects on their craftsmanship, he championed their efforts to integrate "construction and ornament, new technology and ancient forms." Sounds like a blurb for Boston City Hall.

3

The Academy's critical acclaim made KMW celebrities once again. The CEO of pharmaceutical giant Becton Dickinson was so impressed by its metaphorical range and tactile richness that he commissioned the firm to adapt the hut/house/villa idea for their suburban New Jersey headquarters (4). Historical forms and details, abstracted and synthesized, became more conspicuous in their public projects as well, including Boston's Back Bay Station, a Victorian train shed with air shafts reminiscent of Italian campaniles, and the expansion of the nearby Hynes Convention Center, an incipient fortress tamed by loggias and rotundas and grand public rooms overlooking the city.

4

This synthesis of traditional and contemporary elements, abstraction and representation, continues to inform KMW's work, sometimes discreetly, sometimes more literally and emblematically. Both the Young Library at the University of Kentucky and the Fisher School of Business at Ohio State, for example, use vernacular forms and details to connect new buildings, in new parts of campus, to an established architectural order. With the Edward W. Brooke Courthouse and the United States Embassy in Bangkok, on the other

hand, the allusions appear as fragments—a discrete column, a rusticated base, a signature roof detail—that locate the building within a broader architectural context without delivering a homily. Absent is the self-conscious disingenuousness of so many postmodern buildings, which make architecture a secret code decipherable only by the cognoscenti. You don't need a glossary to decipher a KMW building.

KMW's buildings are frequently extensions of the existing city rather than solitary objects in space. "We are essentially urban architects who try to make our buildings part of the fabric," notes Kallmann. "We see architecture as a series of urban pieces, as linkages, one thing connected to the other, rather than as idiosyncratic personal statements." Boston City Hall, dense and self-contained though it seems, was conceived as a continuation of the surrounding urban fabric, with the brick of the city streets becoming the brick of the public plaza, then the floors and walls of the building itself. Originally, a brick passageway ran straight through the base and out the other side. Similarly, the massive Hynes Convention Center is an ode to Boylston Street, sung in a distinctly contemporary key. The Edward W. Brooke Courthouse (5), completed in 2000, mends a fractured urban block while also completing a government complex designed more than 30 years ago by Paul Rudolph. It is simultaneously a piece of city building and an act of homage.

Boston Globe architecture critic Robert Campbell once referred to KMW as "the official civic architects of Boston"; even though the firm's project list now includes laboratories, classroom buildings, and corporate headquarters, that description holds up. Their work displays a dignity and seriousness of purpose associated with civic architecture, but usually without the bombast. Dignity is as much a matter of attitude as scale, a willingness to fit in rather than take over, to do what is required without straining for special effects. KMW's projects are confidently and handsomely built, with respect for the integrity of materials and construction, and a disdain for gratuitous form making. Brick, stone, metal, and glass, nothing appears cheap or thrown together; even modest buildings, such as the Dudley Street Library in Roxbury, have a solidity and sense of permanence that camouflage their skimpy budgets. Yet all this gravitas should not be confused with stuffiness or predictability. Many of KMW's buildings have a certain counter-intuitive quality, a playful ambiguity that suggests that perfection, architectural and otherwise, is neither possible nor perhaps desirable. The surprises come in various forms: the implausible entry column in Harvard's Shad Hall, the dramatic inverted pyramid of Boston City Hall, the beefy arched entry to Harvard's Hauser Hall that is centered not on the façade, as we might expect, but on a slightly deflected allee of trees in front. Even the minimalist Arrow International Headquarters in Pennsylvania (6), with its crisp geometry and refined brickwork, contains canted staircases and telescoping porticos that scramble first impressions. Such details are pop quizzes for the slack-eyed, proof that the quick read is not enough and that full satisfaction requires full attention.

KMW started out in a succession of small walk-up offices near Beacon Hill and the Massachusetts State House, then gradually migrated west to its present location in the eccentric but eminently civilized Tennis and Racquet Club at 939 Boylston Street. The combination of this office on this street, a cross-section of Boston urbanism from H. H. Richardson to Philip Johnson and I. M. Pei, says a lot about KMW. It is a city firm, a downtown firm, a firm aware of history yet comfortable with change, and not preoccupied with projecting a flashy image. To reach the office you have to walk past a Mexican restaurant and through a frequently stuck iron gate, then up worn marble stairs to a front door framed by honor rolls of court tennis and racquet champions dating back to the 19th century.

Over the years, the firm has expanded from five to 80 or more depending on what commissions came through the door. Gerhard Kallmann, now 88, serves as critic emeritus, philosophical sounding board, and institutional memory. "Soul is Gerhard's province," notes one partner. He and Michael McKinnell, 67, still work facing one another across an avalanche of butter paper, like figures in a turn-of-the-century sepia print of an atelier. Both leave CAD to the bright young graduates from Harvard and MIT, who seek out the firm because it is still run by designers, not MBAs. Yet unlike the Pei or Foster offices, in which some senior partners are as prominent as the founders, KMW remains a more or less genial patriarchy, in which Michael McKinnell directs the major projects and indirectly everything else. That could be changing, however. A recent $500 million competition for a research campus for Howard Hughes Medical Institute (7) forced the firm out of the hierarchical studio mode into a more collaborative process. "It was the first time we had ever presented ourselves as a team," says McKinnell. "The complexity of the program required it, but it was also a real learning experience." The office has not been quite the same since. Civic architecture remains the emotional heart of KMW's practice, complemented by college and university buildings, research laboratories, and an occasional corporate headquarters. It is currently designing its first major art museum—the Jack C. Blanton Museum of Art at the University of Texas in Austin—and is constantly on the lookout for an opportunity to design a church, chapel, or other sacred space. The firm has been remarkably lucky in its clients, working consistently for institutions, foundations, corporations, and public agencies with serious social agendas. Consequently, they've not had to rely on motels, shopping centers, and other developer work to keep the lights on and the desks occupied. KMW started out when architects were confident about their place in the grand scheme of things. Modernism was still the acknowledged high road, and social engagement a given. The past was fine but the future was the place to be. Early on, the firm benefited from the shock value of Boston City Hall. They were the bad boys in a very proper town, architects of a bold new building in a bland architectural decade. Now that shock has become a cliché and a bore, reticence, restraint, and craftsmanship are making a comeback.

7

"We've lost interest in shock and radical change," says Michael McKinnell. "These days, the idea of continuity, of bringing things just a little further along, offering a kind of assurance and sense of tradition, has become much more important." If this statement sounds restrained for the architects of Boston City Hall, it also reaffirms some of the values of classic modernism, in which formal expressiveness was usually tempered by sensitivity to proportion, scale, and decorum. It emphasizes the value of responding to whatever lies around, whether existing buildings, or the landscape, or people's memories and enthusiasms. It describes everything that falls under the heading "appropriate and fitting."

# Themes & Variations

The intention of the body of work represented here by some 60 buildings built during 40 years of our firm's existence, is clearly not that of a canonically assertive architecture or ideological crusade but an open-ended patient search, a readiness to expand the formal range of the buildings by the encounter with each new program, site, and client requirements. Our own growth as designers, apart from the stimulus of a continued academic activity at Harvard maintained over many years, depended on the experience of each built project, the insights gained from a series of remarkable clients, and our contact with the technicians and craftsmen involved in the building process. The somewhat erratic flow of a practicing architect's commissions was balanced by undertaking a number of invited or open competitions, leading at times to important built projects.

In an oeuvre which, in a reversal of what is normal, began with its most complex project—the City Hall of 1962—a logical progression or coherent account of architectural development is perhaps difficult to establish. It is possible however to discern in the designs for a great diversity of buildings a perceptible preoccupation with themes which are reworked over time and under different circumstances and which give an undercurrent of continuity to the work.

These have to do with ideas of the linkage of buildings with the urban fabric and the landscape, with architectural history and myth. There is generally the use of a composite order of spaces combining the geometry of Euclidian space with modern flowing space. And there is an emphasis on the poetics of architecture, which transform construction into architectural metaphor.

In the design of the new Boston City Hall, all of these themes were first addressed. The occasion of site, program, and the iconic requirements of a city hall gave us the chance to realize ideas about architecture and the city, which we had developed during a long period of academic study. Ironically, while our interest was essentially in an architecture of urban linkage, the project involved the contradictions of a building which required the finite form of an emblem but also an open-ended extension to the surrounding city fabric signifying the accessibility of modern governance; it also demanded the ambiguities of a language both contemporary and timeless, memorable and long lasting.

The design employed an advanced technology of cast-in-place and pre-cast concrete and a Kahn-like synthesis of structure, services, and architectural form for a tripartite classical composition in brick and concrete. Its realization involved a close cooperation with the brilliant engineer LeMessurier and heroic efforts of construction on a most difficult building site. While the general image of the building made reference to the finite forms of classicism, the public spaces of the interior, the concourse and terraced levels of the mound structure carved into the hillside, as well as the multi-level "forum" of the south hall and courtyard were conceived as extensions of the city's pedestrian network.

The impact of the innovative structure—unlike the deliberate high-tech intrusion of the slightly later design for the Pompidou Museum in Paris—was modified here and enhanced by memories of ancient ramparts, temples, and palazzi, which were equally and paradoxically invoked. Latter-day "deconstructivist" tendencies evident in the fragmented hoods of the façade are in deliberate conflict with the classical columnar order and gravitas of the composition and continue as a resonance of disquiet in much of the work to come.

The recollection of provenance, of prototype and architectural history are underlying themes in many of these designs. There are references, transparent and opaque, to ancient stoas at the Hynes Convention Center, to classical villa and Arts and Crafts architecture at the Academy and Becton Dickinson, to Victorian train sheds at the Back Bay Station, Richardsonian architecture at Hauser Hall, and to the iconic column proposed by Loos for the Chicago Tribune Competition in the design of the Cleveland Courthouse. Such subtexts, while never made unduly explicit, add a play of allusion to the complexity of the designs. In some of the university buildings, such analogues may be more pronounced and part of an aesthetic strategy, which for the sake of stylistic coherence of the campus runs the risk of mimesis or replication.

With regard to the exterior boundaries of the building, there is a general preference for composite, open-ended forms, which capture rather than displace external space. Instead of the reductive minimalism of modern universal space, a complex spatial organization is used inside most of the buildings, combining a classical geometry of space and enclosure with the freedom and asymmetry of modern infinite space. Frequently the order of the spaces is challenged by incidents of topography, the geometries of the site and its movement systems, which introduce a disjunction of angled spaces into the orthogonal Euclidian system. Enfilades of formal rooms are contrasted at times with labyrinthine, complex spatial arrangements, and meandering or axial routes of passage with spaces of stasis. Often a peripheral megaron-type organization surrounds interior space of atria reaching for daylight. The range of the spatial repertoire is further expanded by the landform-related fan-like spaces of the Aaltoesque Pennsylvania residence and the Kauffman Foundation.

Images of shelter and construction are the defining themes of an architectural language which is both abstract and representational. While in the early work images of structure are dominant, they are, in the buildings that follow, absorbed into a tectonic assemblage of wall and opening, portals, aedicule, and sheltering roof overhangs. The identification and celebration of structure itself, as in high-tech, never was the intention, rather its metaphorical use and transformation which early on shows up in the quasi-monastic ambulatory and laced tree-like columns of Phillips Exeter. Although the integration of structure and services into the formal syntax of the building, achieved in the City Hall, is later no longer pursued with the same single-mindedness, construction-based tectonic concerns of load and load bearing, of gravitas, materiality and the assembly of pieces continue to affect the physiognomy of the design. In the more lyrical architecture of the Academy, Becton Dickinson, Arrow, and university buildings, and in response to the context of a particular landscape or a campus, traditional materials of brick and stone are added to the palette of the architectural language. The contemporary use of masonry, no longer weight bearing, but as an outer layer hung on a concealed interior structure, is made evident in the expressive corners of Becton Dickinson where the walls part and the column stands revealed. Increasingly, structure-related forms become a mythical representation, a metaphorical fiction. In the atria of Becton Dickinson columns released from the walls and a minimal truss delineate a rudimentary icon of shelter which invests the space with an aura of ritual. At the Academy a ceremony of columns is representational and iconic rather than structural, and so is the anthropomorphism of single columns standing as sentinels at the entries of Shad Hall and Carnegie Mellon.

In the end, the "high game" is about the vision of an ideal platonic order in conflict with an imperfect, flawed world, where circumstances of topography, site, and human behavior distort and humanize the perfection of an inviolate system. This is made evident in the mannerist collision of opposites, of ceremony and informality, wholeness and fragmentation, composition and disjunction, clarity and enigma, the serene and the awesome, and accounts for complex images of an architecture which resists any easy resolution.

There is little involvement here with the obsessions of the moment, no intention to exploit contemporary anxiety by images of excessive formal gesturing, nor a desire for the excitements of the theme park or the delirium of the shopping mall. Rather, our efforts are concerned with the authenticity of architectural images which, for all their contradictions, are affirmative of contemporary life and its institutions, and essentially optimistic.
—G.M.K. & N.M.McK

# Beginnings

1

At the unveiling of the winning entry in the 1962 Boston City Hall competition, a stunned Mayor John Collins stared at the model for a few moments, then turned to an aide and asked, "What the hell is that?" He might also have asked, "And who the hell are these architects?"

Gerhard Kallmann and Michael McKinnell were then two unknown academics who had thought much and built nothing until they won the most important American public building commission in 50 years. Their design, an inverted pyramid of concrete and brick that was formally inventive and metaphorically resonant, trumped half a dozen prosaic submissions by larger and more established firms.

The 1950s had been a bleak decade for civic design, as though architects suffered collective amnesia about how to make public buildings engaging and memorable. Post offices looked like factories and warehouses, courthouses became indistinguishable from apartment blocks. KMW ignored these dreary precedents with a design that was both ancient and modern, part Kahn and Le Corbusier, part classical temple and palace. "Never since the fall of Knossos have municipal workers been housed in such labyrinthine quarters," noted one perceptive reviewer.

Although Boston City Hall is a neo-Brutalist icon, a grand period piece, it also articulates key themes of KMW's later work. The pedestal, the piano nobile, the monumental façade and ceremonial atrium, the celebration of circulation and structure, the elaborate interplay between light and heavy, open and closed, public and private, all reappear in different guises over the next three decades.

The chairman of the Boston City Hall building commission was Robert Morgan, president of the Boston Five Cents Savings Bank and subsequently an enthusiastic patron of architecture. In 1964, he organized a small competition for an addition to the bank's headquarters at Washington and School streets in downtown Boston (1). Kallmann McKinnell & Wood's winning design adapted elements of City Hall to the scale of a dense city block.

Whereas the original bank building was all wall and Brahmin rectitude, their addition was mostly glass and boldly expressed structure. Eight pairs of split concrete columns, like relics of some ancient forum, create a five-story colonnade that shelters pedestrians while giving the bank an appropriately dignified presence. The curved façade, expressing the shape of the site, also allowed construction of a small public plaza across the street.

2

The Boston Five was followed by the Woodhull Medical Center in Brooklyn, another structural tour de force with 68-foot trusses and interstitial floors, the glass block Dudley Street Library in Roxbury, and the Athletics Facility at Phillips Exeter Academy in New Hampshire (**2**). Here Brutalist rawness found lyrical expression amidst the red brick and ancestral elms of a venerable prep school. Although architectural concrete was once again the material of choice, the architects used exposed steel trusses to support the roof, giving the entire structure a springy, gymnastic quality. Motion and mass in a spirited tug-of-war, and several years before the exoskeletal splash of Piano and Rogers' Centre Pompidou in Paris.

The Athletics Facility was under construction at the same time as Louis Kahn's Exeter Library — the Leonardo of architectural concrete and an aspiring disciple working only a few hundred yards from one another. Yet Kahn's building, located in the center of campus, is wrapped in traditional red brick, whereas KMW's, hovering on the periphery, is all bones and muscle. Of the branching concrete columns in the center's spine, Kahn reportedly commented, "I would have made them planes with holes."

By the time the building opened in 1970, Brutalism's moment had passed. Raw confrontational architecture was rapidly giving way to more layered and historically resonant buildings that painted pictures and told stories. Robert Venturi's *Complexity and Contradiction in Architecture* had replaced Le Corbusier's *Vers une Architecture Nouveau* as the canonical text. The message to Kallmann McKinnell & Wood was unmistakable: change course or sink.

# Boston City Hall

BOSTON, MASSACHUSETTS : 1962–68

Located between Faneuil Hall and I.M.Pei's Government Center, City Hall links the old and the new Boston. The contours of Beacon Hill flow through the building, forming the lower public levels that are carved into the hillside, and descend some twenty feet to New Congress Street and the markets. The mayor's office, the council chamber, and the councilors' offices are suspended at the piano nobile level, with four tiered office floors above. This arrangement corresponds to a tripartite classical order, and is clearly and memorably expressed on the exterior of the building by brick volumes, concrete piers, and projecting hoods and fins. Internally, these spaces are linked by an intricate system of staircases, concourses, and atria that celebrate movement and the accessibility of municipal government. The surrounding plaza, a monumental extension of the brick pavement of the historic city, provides a setting for rallies, concerts, and occasional world championships. But a public passage through the courtyard has regrettably been closed, and general maintenance has been deplorable. Still, City Hall conveys a powerful sense of materiality and a clear hierarchy of construction elements. Its dramatic siting and formal complexity reveal a confident, assertive modernism enriched with memories of ancient civic architecture.

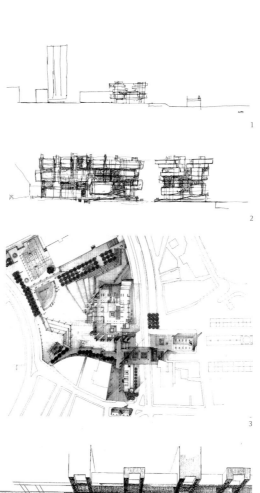

1,2: Early conceptual sketches
3: Site plan of City Hall and
   Government Center Plaza
4: Sketch of lower level
   tiered concourse
5: The east façade
   overlooks Faneuil Hall and
   Quincy Market.

1: City Hall and Custom
    House Tower
2: The tri-partite west façade
3: City Hall Plaza
4: Southwest corner and
    Faneuil Hall

2

3

4

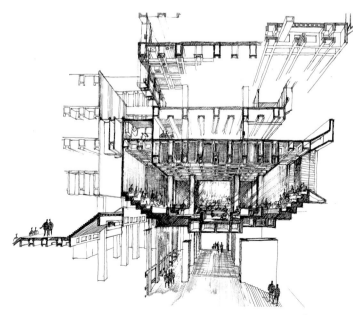

1: Lower level concourse
2: The mayor's office
   overlooking Faneuil Hall
3: Sketch of Council Chamber
   and entrance lobby
4: A grand staircase connects
   the lobby with the offices.

4

# Boston Five Cents Savings Bank

BOSTON, MASSACHUSETTS : 1966–72

At the Boston Five, what might have been a run-of-the-mill addition became a stunning public room, complete with wraparound windows and small foreground plaza. The architects took advantage of an odd but prominent triangular site—created by a street realignment—to design a tall, glassy banking hall that swells out to meet the city. Split concrete columns and radiating post-tensioned beams, again reminiscent of Boston City Hall, form a lofty colonnade that shelters pedestrians and presents an image of dignity and permanence appropriate for a bank. The columnless interior is airy, open, and filled with natural light; at night, it glows like a lantern. The bank has since been converted into a bookstore and cafe that support a different kind of public life.

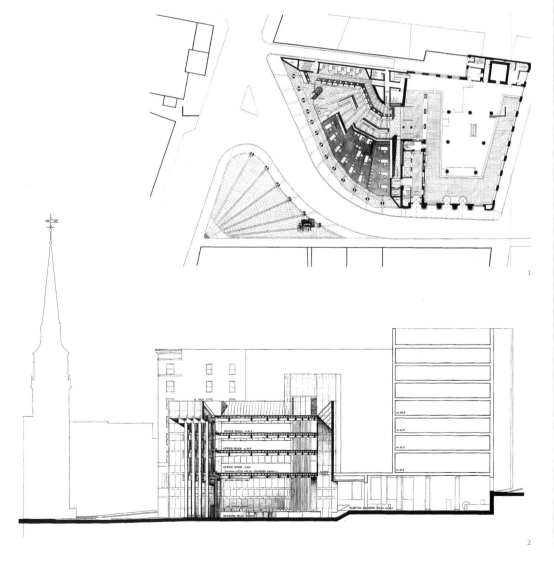

1

2    3

1: Plan of bank and plaza
2: Section through banking hall
   and offices above
3: The glass façade provides the
   building with transparency.

2

3

4

# Phillips Exeter Academy Athletics Facility

EXETER, NEW HAMPSHIRE : 1965–70

From its massive concrete walls and whorled
central atrium to its celebration of structure
and circulation, the athletics facility is the
unmistakable offspring of Boston City Hall.
It is organized around a three-level spine, from
which hockey rinks, squash and basketball
courts, and viewing galleries are directly accessi-
ble. Individual roofs are suspended from tubular
steel trusses that create open, column-free
spaces, while giving the exterior a gymnastic
flourish. The handling of natural light represents
a major advance over City Hall.

A product of the architects' youthful
Brutalist period, the building has aged
handsomely, its steel trusses rusting to the
color of tree trunks. Compared to the typical
mute, monolithic school gymnasium, it is
positively lyrical.

1

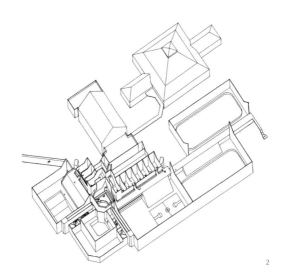

2

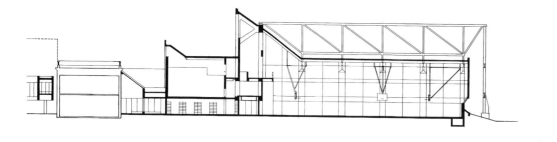

3

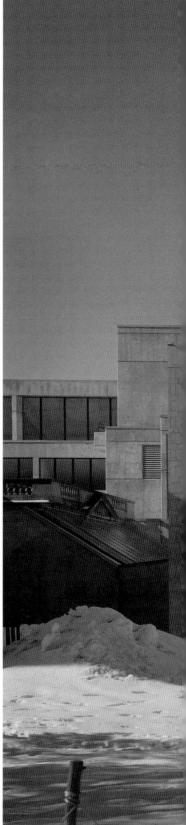

4

1: Site plan of building at
    edge of campus
2: Axonometric
3: Section revealing the
    cathedral-like spine
4: A long entrance ramp leads
    to the mid level entrance.

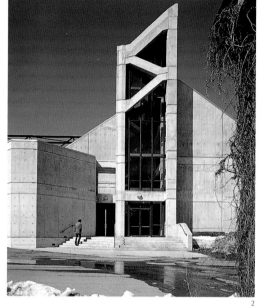

1: Main entrance
2: The spine forms a
   chamfered tower.
3: Triangular steel trusses
   suspend the roof.
4: The trusses and supports
5: Ice rinks flank the concrete
   spine at the visitors' gallery.
6: Central atrium and
   concourse
7: Swimming pool and
   suspended roof

5

6

7

# Parliamentary Office Building Competition

LONDON, ENGLAND : 1971

The architects described their submission in the Parliamentary Office Competition as "a fragment of a large fabric building with the potential for further extension." An integrated urban element, in other words, instead of an autonomous object. The program called for new offices to relieve chronic congestion in the existing quarters at Westminster. KMW proposed an L-shaped structure of traditional Portland stone that turned the corner at Parliament Square and embraced Norman Shaw's picturesque New Scotland Yard. It featured a long narrow arcade lined with shops and connected to an underground tube station. The tight column spacing picks up the rhythm of Sir Charles Barry's and Pugin's neo-Gothic façades of the Houses of Parliament. The new offices wrapped a sky-lit atrium criss-crossed by pedestrian bridges, with terraces offering views across the Thames. But there was little public enthusiasm for the winning design, a massive foursquare volume, and it wasn't until 1998 that a new office building, designed by Sir Michael Hopkins, finally rose on the site.

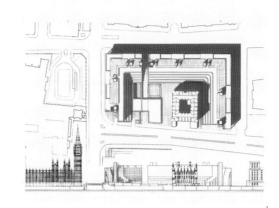

1

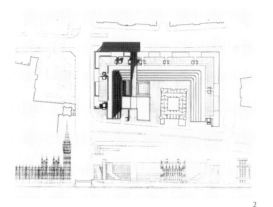

2

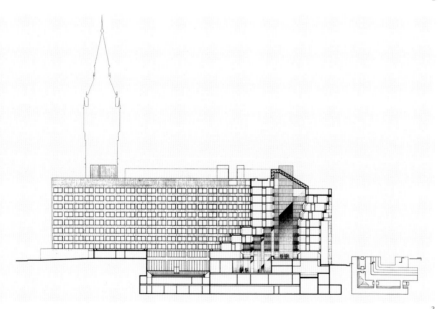

3    4

1: Final site plan envelops
   Norman Shaw's New
   Scotland Yard.
2: First phase plan
3: Section through tall atrium
4: View of first phase
   of construction

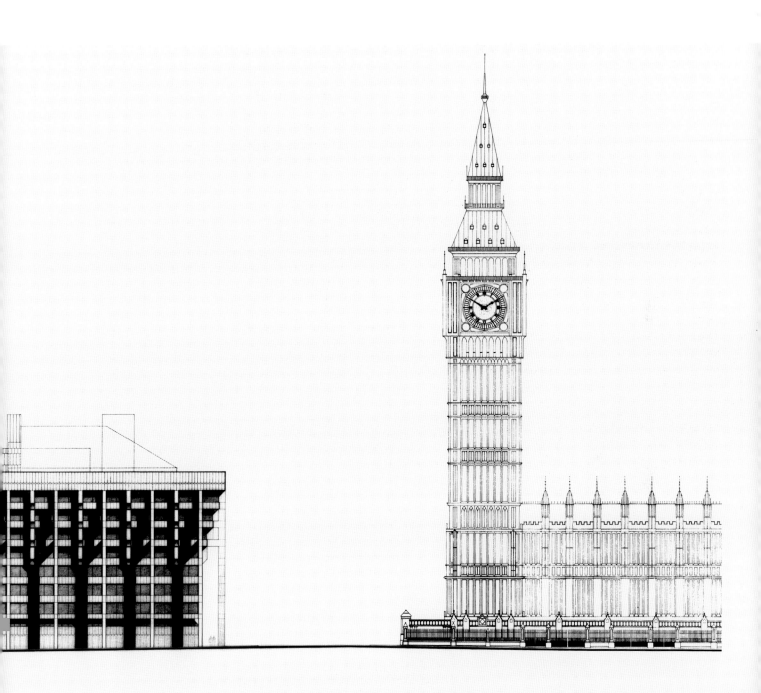

# Buildings and the City

ELEVATION   WEST

2

3

In every city where they have worked—Boston, Cleveland, Washington, Atlanta, Berlin, Singapore—Kallmann McKinnell & Wood have responded instinctively and enthusiastically to the swirl of urban life. They understand that good urban buildings are not superior to their surroundings, that they take their cues from the circumstances at hand rather than the abstractions of the academy. Instead of discrete objects in space, they are parts of an ensemble; rather than formal purity and singleness of purpose, they seek to reinforce the vitality of street, block, and square. Ultimately, they must fit in rather than take over. (**1**)

In both competition projects and completed buildings, KMW has been sensitive to all of these issues. Their 1971 proposal for the Parliamentary office buildings in London (**2**) was a tight L facing the Houses of Parliament and Parliament Street, in the shadow of Big Ben and a short walk from the Thames. Instead of an isolated office block, cut off from the city, they proposed an elegant extrusion featuring a traditional colonnade with shops at street level and links to New Scotland Yard and other nearby government offices. For the United States Embassy in Berlin, Gerhard Kallmann's birthplace, they proposed an intricately layered building straddling the fault line between East and West, adjacent to the Brandenburg Gate. The combination of different geometries— circle, square, rectangle, trapezoid—and distinct architectural languages— classical to modern—reflected the polyglot culture of the city and the complex political and social pressures impinging on the site. (**3**)

Less politically charged, but equally challenging was the firm's 1988 renovation of the Hynes Convention Center in Boston, a ponderous box that added little to the cityscape except bulk (**4**). The architects peeled back the existing building to its structural supports, then introduced loggias, arcades, and shopping pavilions, plus grand public rooms at the top that reminded visitors that they were in Boston, not Buffalo or Omaha. Their efforts revived a moribund stretch of Boylston Street by creating a stunning street wall, a kind of horizontal armature, to which other architects and developers have attached themselves.

Likewise, the starting point for the 1999 Edward W. Brooke Courthouse (**5**) in Boston's Government Center was the opportunity to complete a grand civic design begun more than thirty years earlier by architect Paul Rudolph. The courthouse's shape, materials, and basic organization update and enhance a heroic but flawed scheme, and reconnect it to the city. The Carl Stokes Court House in Cleveland, opened in 2002, is an urban reclamation effort on a grander scale, featuring a dramatic 24-story tower located on a derelict stretch of riverfront. The completion of the main plaza and an adjacent park—both stalled by budget problems—will finally establish the grand ceremonial link between city and courthouse that the architects originally envisioned. (**6**)

Implicit in each of these projects is a recognition that great cities are sedimentary, built up layer by layer over decades and centuries. Good urban architects, therefore, behave like archaeologists, digging beneath quotidian surfaces to uncover bedrock, then re-presenting it in ways that make the city seem comfortably familiar and surprisingly new.

4

5

6

BUILDINGS AND THE CITY : 31

# Back Bay Station

BOSTON, MASSACHUSETTS : 1976–87

With its soaring arches and intricate concrete and glass side walls, Boston's Back Bay Station recalls the majestic train terminals of the 19th and early 20th centuries, one of which it replaced. The concourse is bright and transparent and lined with food stands and flower stalls— as much covered street as building. It bends gently to follow the curve of the tracks below, its laminated roof trusses resting on impossibly small corbels, as though gravity had been temporarily suspended. Except for the campanile-like airshafts at the rear of the site, the station is an essay in implausible lightness that gives the daily commute a touch of romance.

1

2

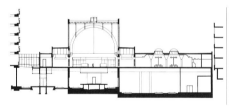

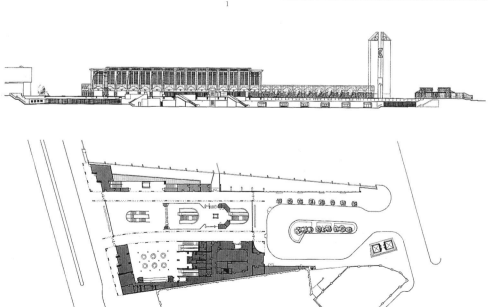

3

4

BACK BAY·SOUTH

5

1: Cross section
2: Sketch of the ventilation shaft
3: Section
4: Plan
5: The soaring arches recall
   19th century train stations.

1

2

3

4

5

6

# Hynes Memorial Convention Center

BOSTON, MASSACHUSETTS : 1983–89

The Hynes Memorial Convention center is a box that became a building and finally a civic icon. Over a period of six years, KMW wrapped an existing shell with an L of arcades, loggias, and heavy variegated stone, blending contemporary and classical elements into a lively polyglot exterior. Inside, visitors move through rotundas and up staircases with unusual ceremoniousness, as though they themselves were the main attraction. Yet unlike most convention centers, which are introverted and solipsistic, these interior spaces are connected to neighboring hotels and shopping malls, turning the entire block into a surrogate town square. The building's signature element is a monumental loggia stretching some 500 feet along historic Boylston Street. Stone arches and large modern windows welcome the public, while on the upper floors tall vaulted galleries present spectacular views of Back Bay and the Boston skyline. Instead of walling out the city, the Hynes Convention Center presents many opportunities to savor it.

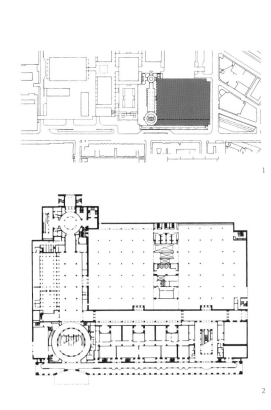

1

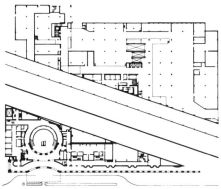

2

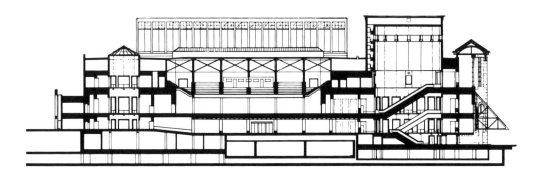

3

4

5

1: Site plan
2, 3: Lower level plan
4: Section
5: View of main frontage on
   Boylston Street

1

2

3

4

5

7

6

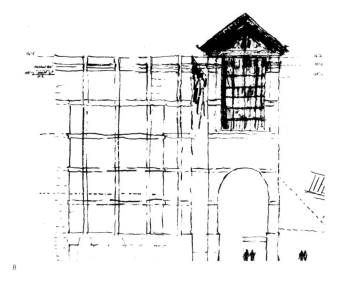

8

1: Break-out space and
   circulation gallery
2: Up view of entrance rotunda
3: Down view of
   entrance rotunda
4: Sketch of ballroom
5: Ballroom interior
6: Sky-lit stair behind
   rotunda wall

# United States Embassy Competition

BERLIN, GERMANY : 1995

The return of the United States Embassy to its prewar location on the historic Pariser Platz, close to the Brandenburg Gate and the Reichstag, demanded an architectural response of unusual complexity. The design had to express the presence and values of the United States, balance the competing demands of accessibility and security, and recognize both the city's neoclassical heritage and its desire for modernity. The proposed scheme is a collage of urban pieces: a chancery pavilion, a wedge-shaped consular hall, an obliquely angled office compound with a central courtyard, and a linear orangery. The interplay of basic geometries—circle, square, rectangle, and trapezoid—is complemented by the interplay of different architectural languages. The formal classicism of the chancery spaces contrasts with the contemporary openness and fluidity of the office wing and the technological panache of the courtyard enclosure. The embassy's short entry façade responds to the stylistic restrictions of the Pariser Platz with a fractured classical composition and a window feature that recalls a Schinkel palais that stood nearby. The façades facing the Tiergarten and the Holocaust Memorial site use a stone-banded modern grid as a compositional matrix. Past and present, memory and invention talking to one another on the most symbolically important site in Berlin.

2

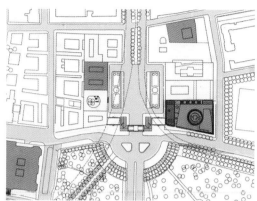

3

4

5

1

6

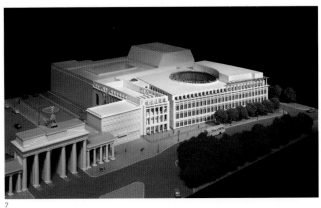

7

8

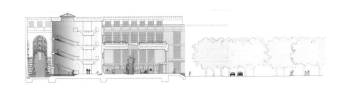

9

10

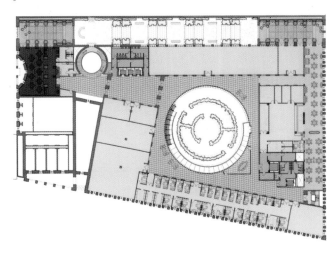

11

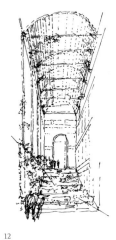

12

13

14

# United States Embassy

BANGKOK, THAILAND : 1988–96

Bangkok is synonymous with lushness, and in its design for the United States Embassy KMW underscored this quality, while still presenting an appropriately dignified face in a foreign land. The embassy consists of a long, five-story administration building, and a smaller entry pavilion containing the key ceremonial spaces. The office wing is dense and bunker-like, with massive walls and small square windows; the pavilion, on the other hand, is more open and welcoming thanks to a loggia with tall windows and terraces that look out on an enclosed water garden. A residence for the ambassador and a second office building is to complete the compound, which possesses many of the qualities of a tropical villa. All buildings are finished in the white marble and stucco typical of buildings in Bangkok.

1

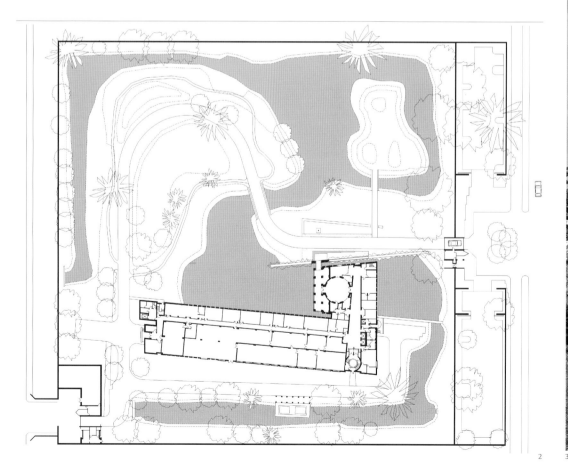

2    3

1: Site context
2: The embassy is set back from
   the road for security reasons.
3: Pavilion and office wing

1: Building with traditional
   klong.
2: White marble and stucco
   are typical of Bangkok's
   public buildings.
3: The entry pavilion
4: Downview of water garden
   and pavilion terrace
5: Office
6: Cafeteria

4

5

6

# OPCW World Headquarters

THE HAGUE : 1993–98

The headquarters of the Organisation for the
Prohibition of Chemical Weapons is located at
Catsheuvel, a prominent site between J.J.P Oud's
Netherlands Congress Hall and Berlage's City Art
Museum. As in the Stokes United States Court
House in Cleveland, the architects combined
curved and orthogonal forms to respond to
different site conditions and to reflect the organization's global mission. From the boulevard, the
building is a graceful cylinder with regular stacks
of windows and an assertive metal cornice. This
configuration opens up views of Oud's Congress
Hall and tower at the rear of the site.

On the garden side, however, the curve
intersects a rectangular bar of offices, which at
the ground level serves as the delegates' lounge
and connects to the rotated square of the
executive council chamber. The orthogonals pick
up the grid of the adjacent neighborhood;
similarly, the curved façade is covered in a pale
brick, like many boulevard buildings, while
the garden façade is finished in the buff tones
that predominate in the older city.

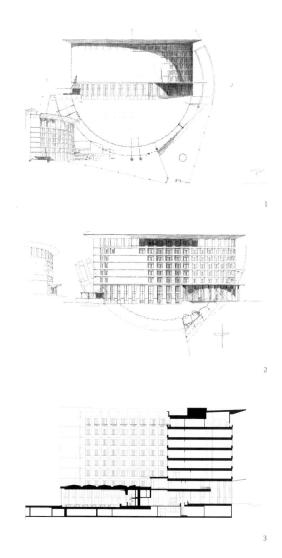

1

2

3

1, 2, 3: Volumetric studies
and section
4: Ground floor and site plan
5: The curving façade creates
a distinctive image on
the boulevard

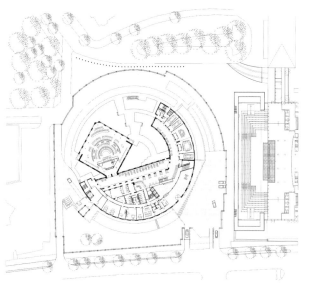

4    5

1: The concave façade and
   the council chamber pavilion
   and garden
2, 3: Views from the Boulevard
4: Entrance and Oud's
   Netherlands Congress
   Hall Tower
5, 6, 7: Delegates' lounge
8: Council chamber

4

5

6

7

8

# Edward W. Brooke Courthouse

BOSTON, MASSACHUSETTS : 1993–99

The Edward W. Brooke Courthouse fills out an odd triangular site in Boston's Government Center, pushing to the street on two sides and providing a tall colonnade on the third, where it meets Paul Rudolph's State Services Center, an unfinished tour de force from the late 1960s that is both astonishing and alienating.

The courthouse was designed to complete that earlier complex, using different materials and iconography but preserving the civic scale. Its crisp lines and smooth stone façade play against Rudolph's curved forms, which are finished in rough striated concrete. Visitors enter at the tip of the triangle, pass through a security checkpoint, and ascend a grand staircase to a four-story atrium, the building's most dramatic feature. A second entry opposite the first leads to a lofty arcade and a shared landscape courtyard. All are washed in natural light from clerestories and corridor windows, some of which provide glimpses of the Boston skyline.

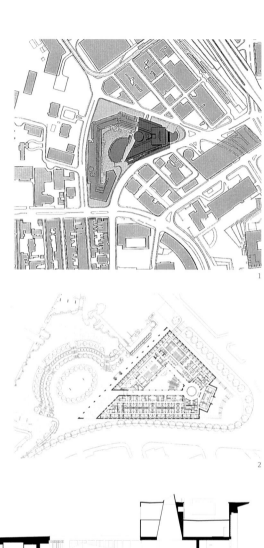

1

2

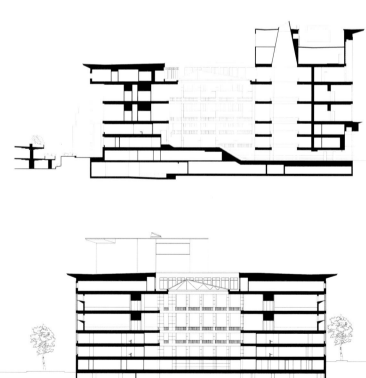

3

4    5

1: Site plan
2: Ground floor plan
3, 4: Sections through atrium
5: A four-story arcade connects
   two city streets

1

1: View of the State Services
   Center from the arcade
2: The classicized portico of
   the main entrance
3, 4: The arcade responds to
   the monumental scale of
   the Rudolph building.
5: Passage through the site
   between the two buildings

2

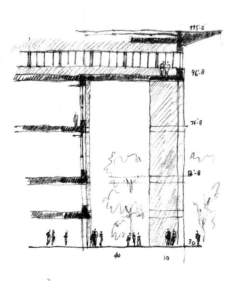

3

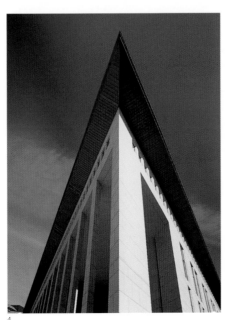

4

5

1: Entrance rotunda
2: Door detail
3: Courtroom
4: Judge's chamber
5: Courtrooms are entered
   from galleries surrounding
   the central atrium.

5

# Carl B. Stokes United States Court House

CLEVELAND, OHIO : 1994–2003

With its cylindrical form and dramatic cornice, the Carl B. Stokes Court House has become an instant landmark in downtown Cleveland. The curved façade overlooks the Cuyahoga River, from which it resembles a shield, while the narrower rectilinear pieces face downtown. This blending of curved and orthogonal forms recalls the OPCW Headquarters in The Hague, though at a dramatically different scale. All façades are covered in a lattice of limestone and marble that adds appealing depth and texture. Visitors enter at the southwest corner, beneath a monumental figure of Venus by Jim Dine, then pass into a rotunda and lobby with spectacular views of the city and the river. The courtrooms on the upper floors, like those in the Brooke Courthouse in Boston, are bathed in natural light. The interiors, mostly drywall and vinyl, are frugal but quietly elegant.

1

2

5

1: The court house adds a
   distinctive form to the
   city prospect.
2: Rendering showing the
   court house and the
   Cuyahoga River
3, 4: The curved façade faces
   the river.
5: Sections

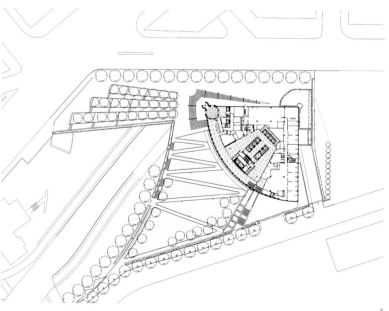

3

4

1: View of court house
   framed by 19th century
   masonry buildings
2: View from river
3, 4: Corner and sculpture

2

3

4

1: Courtroom
2: Entrance rotunda
3: Main lobby
4: Public lobby and stairs
   to library

4

# World Trade Center West

BOSTON, MASSACHUSETTS : 1998–2003

This is the third of three mid-rise towers on Boston's World Trade Center Pier, part of an ambitious redevelopment of the city's historic waterfront. In addition to a hotel and an office tower—designed by different architects— KMW's competition-winning office building includes underground parking for 350 cars and a fan-shaped park with pavilions for a café and day care center. A broad exterior stair, decorated with a sea serpent sculpture, links the park and the waterfront. The slight curve in the building's façade softens its orthogonal geometry while opening up views of the harbor. The masonry volumes allude to the beefy warehouses and fishing piers along the waterfront, while the light metal construction of the lower structures suggests the world of modern technology, subtly underscoring the shift from old economy to new that is the heart of Boston's current renaissance.

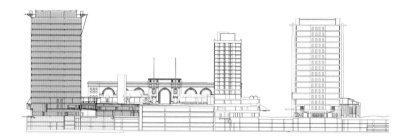

1

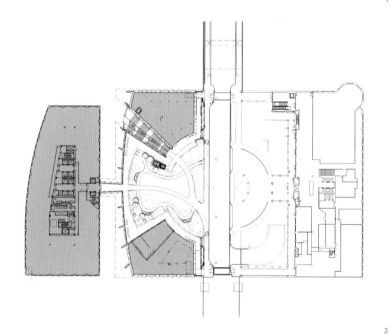

2

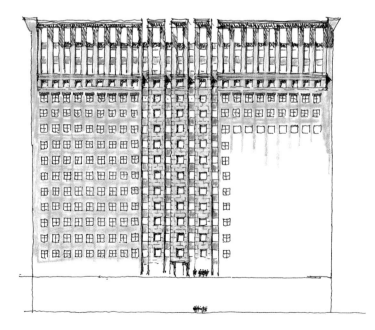

1: Site section
2: Site plan
3: Study of east elevation
4: View of the harbor-
  facing façade

3

4

1

2

3

4

5

1: The lower pavilions and
staircase leading to a garden
terrace above
2, 3: Upper level with view
of harbor and garden
4: Wind mitigation "sails" and
trellis canopy of podium
structure with masonry wall
of the office tower.

4

# Buildings and the Landscape

Although Kallmann McKinnell & Wood are known as urban architects, and certainly consider themselves such, some of their best buildings are in rural or semi-pastoral settings. The American Academy of Arts and Sciences, for example, allowed the firm to explore the relationships between landscape and architecture for the first time. Before, landscape had been largely tangential, a grace note, or merely what was left over when a building was completed. Now it became a source of image, idea, and form. The shift was not ideological, a conscious decision either to merge or decisively separate building and setting, but circumstantial. The clients knew what they wanted, but had no idea what form it should take. That opened the door to experimentation.

Starting conceptually as a blend of archetypal hut and columnar temple, the Academy evolved into a simple pyramid that became an extension and culmination of a hill, then into a combination classical villa and turn-of-the-century New England country house nestled among trees (1). Here and there the landscape was allowed to nibble away at the building's foundation, providing a suggestive metaphor for devouring time.

Kallmann McKinnell & Wood had never worked at such an intimate domestic scale, or used brick, stone, wood, and copper so generously. The result was critically acclaimed and, to the firm's surprise, financially rewarding. Becton Dickinson executives Jack Howe and William Nolen were so impressed that they hired KMW to design their new headquarters in Franklin Lakes, New Jersey (2). Edwin Land's memorable description of the Academy, "a trysting place where great minds can copulate," could stand as a capsule summary of the Becton Dickinson program. They too wanted an intellectual "trysting place" that fostered collaboration and the disinterested pursuit of ideas without the usual corporate distractions. So instead of flashing signs and declamatory gates, Becton Dickinson got a narrow entry drive that meanders through woods and meadows to a stream at the base of a gentle hill. Poussin again, but without the ruins. Even the parking garages are tucked discreetly into the hillside.

Before design began, Becton Dickinson hired Boston landscape architect Morgan Wheelock to help them choose a site and determine its basic relationship to the future buildings. He proposed a series of simple shed forms that reached out like fingers toward meadows and a sweeping central lawn. (The digital plan recurs in the Kauffman Foundation Building in Kansas City and, in abridged form, at the private residence in Reading, Pennsylvania.) Instead of buildings being imposed on the land, the land effectively designed the buildings. "We were creating a garden," Wheelock explains, "and the buildings were masses of stone that fixed the walls of those spaces." It is as close as American corporate architecture has come to Vaux.

Wheelock and KMW teamed up again on the Arrow International Headquarters in Reading, Pennsylvania (**3**), a leaner and cleaner type of corporate villa that fit the needs of a young company on the rise. Shed roofs and manicured gardens gave way to Aaltoesque brick forms set in rolling farmland. This time, offices, laboratories, and manufacturing spaces all occupy the same building, which looks out on an undulating landscape of forests and farms. Large square windows frame views of the site; even the tall entry portico pulls the eye through the building to the landscape beyond, as though one were an extension of the other.

Although Becton Dickinson is richer and more evocative, Arrow set the tone for many future KMW buildings. The taut line of descent from it to the OPCW Headquarters in The Hague and the recent Federal Food and Drug Administration building in Washington is unmistakable. The villa motif recurs in more exotic form in the United States Embassy in Bangkok, the centerpiece of which is an enclosed water garden filled with native plants. While the architecture evokes the city's historic buildings, the plan itself celebrates the ancient ecology of the site.

One of the clearest, and most classically modern, fusions of building and landscape occurs at the De Cordova Museum in Lincoln, Massachusetts (**4**). Here a simple brick-and-glass box is set into a terraced hillside, its grand staircase responding directly to the fall of the land. The building's compact vertical form is urban, but the experience is decidedly pastoral. As visitors move from level to level, they enjoy unobstructed views of the surrounding sculpture park, which seems about to push through the side of the museum.

3

4

# American Academy of Arts and Sciences

CAMBRIDGE, MASSACHUSETTS : 1977–81

The American Academy of Arts and Sciences occupies the former site of Shady Hill, the stately home of Boston's first mayor. Originally proposed for the lower half of the lot, it was subsequently moved to the top of the hill. In its forms and details, the Academy recalls the work of Frank Lloyd Wright, Greene and Greene, and numerous other architects; yet its roots go further back to Delphi, the ancient academies, and Abbe Laugier's famous drawing of the primitive hut. These sources are expressed quietly and obliquely—as a colonnade, a series of wooden roof brackets, or a bit of vegetation encroaching on a corner of the building. One of the Academy's strengths is the way it synthesizes so many historical details without devolving into a pastiche. It is restrained, dignified, and internally mysterious, like an ideogram for the questing mind. The client, represented by Polaroid founder Edwin Land, physicist Victor Weisskopf, and historian Thomas Boylston Adams, played a pivotal role in refining the design.

2

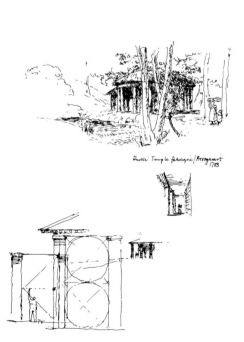

3

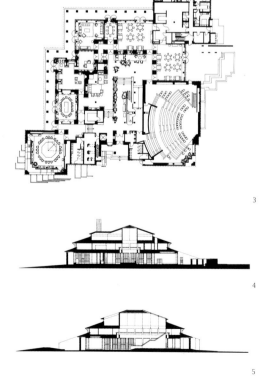

4

5

6

1: West façade
2, 3: Colonnade
4: Sketch of brick column
   and wood superstructure
5: View from south

3

4

5

1: Entrance hall
2: Garden room
3: Fireplace
4: Library
5: Conference room
6: Lecture amphitheater
7: Atrium and stairs

7

# Asian Export Wing, Peabody-Essex Museum

SALEM, MASSACHUSETTS : 1984–88

This 30,000-square-foot addition to Salem's Peabody-Essex Museum is an epitome of ideas and motifs found in many KMW buildings: the atrium, the ceremonial staircase, the layering of modern and historical elements. The façade of the new wing frames an existing Chinese garden, integrating a planar brick wall with a moongate and tiled roof typical of Oriental shrines. Visitors pass from the garden to a series of varied exhibition galleries containing porcelain, jade, scrimshaw, and other staples of the 19th-century Asia trade. A spiral wooden staircase, executed in the spirit of Salem master Samuel McIntire, connects the three exhibition floors. Between the new wing and the adjoining 1824 East India Marine Hall the architects inserted a tall narrow atrium to mark the transition from old to new, and also to expose the handsome façade of the historic trading hall.

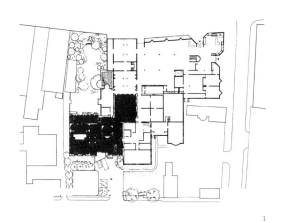

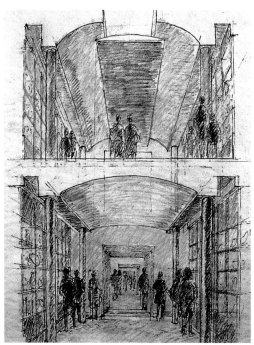

1

2

3    4

1: Plan of Asian Export Wing
   and garden
2: Sketch of atrium and
   restored façade
3: Sketch of galleries
4: Garden façade

1: Main staircase
2: Section through galleries
3: Octagonal gallery
4: View into staircase
5: Sketch of staircase
6: Atrium

3

4

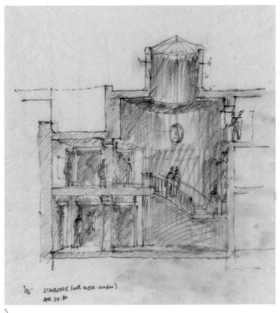

⁵⁄₁₆" STAIRCASE (with mezz-window)
APR 24 84

5

6

# Becton Dickinson I & II

FRANKLIN LAKES, NEW JERSEY : 1981–92

The directors of Becton Dickinson, the world's largest manufacturer of bandages, thermometers, and other medical supplies, wanted a corporate headquarters that was quietly memorable and emphatically non-hierarchical, where collaboration among researchers, technicians, and marketers was a priority instead of an accident.

Working closely with Boston landscape architect Morgan Wheelock, KMW designed a group of long two- and three-story buildings that reach out to adjacent meadows, woods, and ponds, creating a harmonious integration of structure and setting. The use of pitched roofs, French doors, and other domestic details further reinforces the corporate villa motif. Parking garages, the curse of the suburban landscape, are screened or tucked into hillsides to preserve the site's rural character. Building I, completed in 1986, is organized around a series of dramatic atria: a formal hemicycle in the executive suite, a sculpture hall, and an interior garden with an archaeological abstraction by Michael Singer for the office wings. The finger-like plan allows most offices to be located on exterior walls, with rich natural light and carefully framed views of woods, gardens, and the central Great Lawn. The second building, which opened in 1992, includes laboratories, offices, and support spaces, and is consequently more subdued and businesslike than its predecessor; except for the atria, which resemble elaborate stage sets awaiting the actors. Yet once again, landscape is as important as architecture, supplying the connective tissue that holds the structural skeleton together.

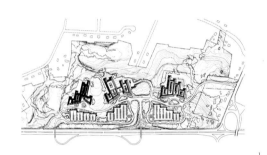

1

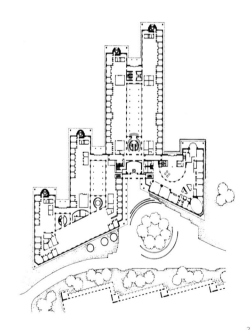

2

3    4

1: Site plan
2: Ground floor plan of the
   corporate headquarters
3: Elevation
4: The low shed-like buildings
   defer to the landscape.

1: Entrance and reflecting pool
2: Southwest corner and parking screen wall
3: View from great lawn
4: Garden terrace
5: Up-view of corner
6: Main atrium and sculpture garden
7: Stairs and view into atrium
8: Executive atrium and column

1

2

3

4

5

6

7

8

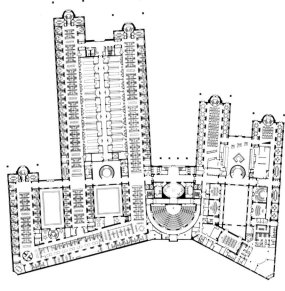

3

4

5

6

# Arrow International Headquarters

READING, PENNSYLVANIA : 1989–91

Arrow International is a minimalist version
of a corporate villa on the outskirts of Reading,
Pennsylvania. A circular entry drive passes
through remnants of meadows and hedgerows to
a curved brick façade that is as much garden
wall as entrance. Immediately behind are one-
story laboratories and manufacturing spaces—
the company makes and packages medical
products—followed by a three-story atrium
with tall clerestory windows bringing light to the
suspended office floors. A tall glazed entry
portico slices through one end of the building,
narrowing slightly as it goes so that the eye is
carried past the rear wall to a rolling meadow in
the distance. For all that, the basic design is
direct and pragmatic, the result of a tight budget
and an accelerated construction schedule. And
even though it includes such familiar KMW
flourishes as a swooping roof and a cantilevered
cornice, its strength resides in the clarity and
refinement of its brickwork, some of the best the
firm has produced.

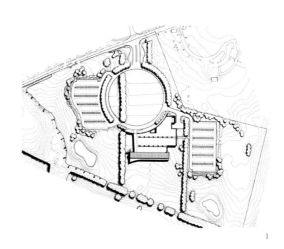

1

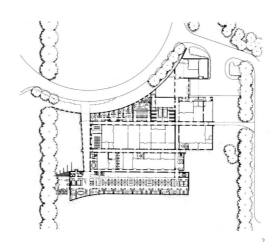

2

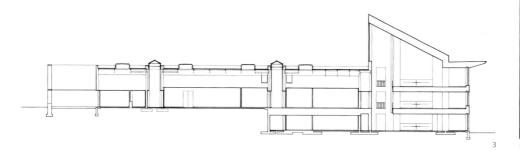

3

4

1: Site plan
2: Site and ground floor plan
3: Section
4: Northwest corner of
   office wing

1: Meadow and building from entrance drive
2: The curved entrance wall becomes a garden wall
3: North façade
4: Entrance portico
5: Opening in the garden wall
6: Suspended office floors and atrium
7: Work station
8: Office and view

6

7

8

# The Getty Villa Museum Competition

MALIBU, CALIFORNIA : 1993

The need for added facilities and improved access to the grounds of the Getty Villa at Malibu is met by a design proposal which leaves the existing faithful reconstruction of a famous first-century Roman villa and garden untouched, but provides it with a dramatic new context of building and landscape involving significant changes to the movement pattern of visitors. The villa is now entered from a colonnaded trapezoidal forum with chambers for the new facilities (a plaster-cast gallery, museum shop, lecture hall, restaurant) carved into the hill on the west and north side. Visitors and their cars are directed to a shaded parking space on an elevated plateau from which the villa and its gardens can be viewed. From here a staircase and elevator cut into a steep ravine alongside a water channel (shades of Tivoli) descend into the forum as if into an archaeological site. The development of the grounds maps out an episodic journey in the manner of picturesque gardens, with paths following the contours and features such as footbridges, waterfall, sculpture garden and exedra, and an amphitheater and belvedere located on the hilltop. The evocation of themes recalling the partial excavation of the villa in the late 18th century and the composition of architectural fragments and landscape reminiscent of Claude Lorraine, add another dimension of perception to a remarkable if problematical historical reconstruction.

2

4

3

5

6

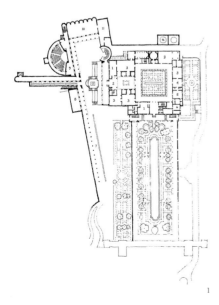

1

1: Plan of the villa, forum,
   and extensions
2: View of the villa from
   Belvedere
3: Forum, plaster cast gallery,
   and grand stair
4: Ravine and stair
5: Sculpture garden
6: Forum and fountain
7: Upview from the forum

8: Ravine, footbridge, and villa
9: Site plan

7

8

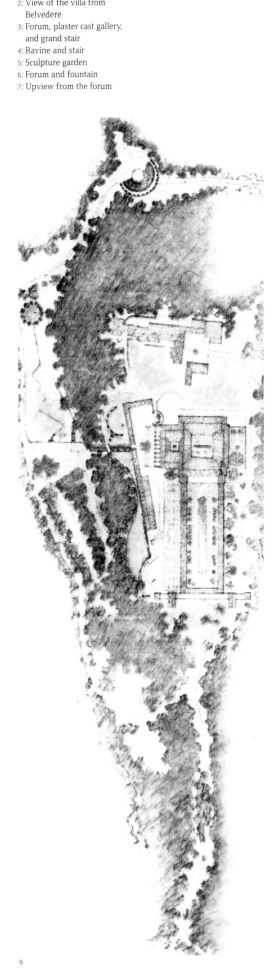

9

# Private Residence

BERKS COUNTY, PENNSYLVANIA : 1993–97

The refined brick detailing of Arrow International reappears in this expansive home, one of only two residences KMW has designed. The plan is a simple U, with a large living room at the center and broad terrace featuring a reclining Henry Moore sculpture. The terrace is framed by two shed-like wings containing the main living spaces as well as a series of galleries for displaying the owner's extensive collection of contemporary art and ceramics. The wings get taller as they reach out into the landscape, producing handsome framed views of the countryside. The combination of maple floors, mahogany ceilings and window frames, gray slate, and water-struck brick creates an atmosphere of subdued elegance.

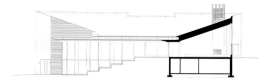

1

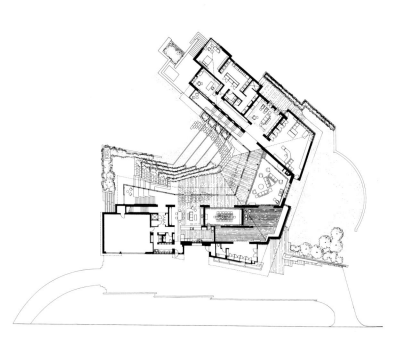

2

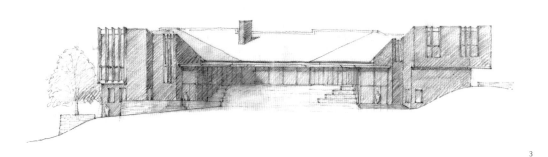

3

4

1: Section
2: Ground floor plan
3: Elevation sketch
4: The low spreading house
   settles into the landscape.

1: Night view of entrance
2: Northwest corner
3: View from west
4: Gallery
5: Dining room
6: Studio
7: Gallery and entrance
8: Living room
9: Stair and gallery

4

5

6

7

8

9

# DeCordova Museum

LINCOLN, MASSACHUSETTS : 1992–98

The original DeCordova estate was an eccentric
pile of brick towers and battlements perched on
a small hill in a fashionable Boston suburb.
Charming from a distance, its quirky spaces and
inscrutable circulation proved to be a curatorial
nightmare. KMW's 11,500-square-foot exhibition hall solved both problems. The addition
stairsteps gracefully down the steep hillside,
selectively abstracting the decorative details of
the original building, while connecting it to the
museum school and parking lot below. The
central organizing element is a glazed staircase
that intersects galleries at every level, and also
gives visitors unobstructed views of the surrounding sculpture park, the museum's most
popular feature.

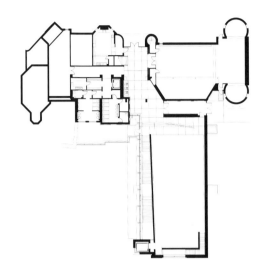

1

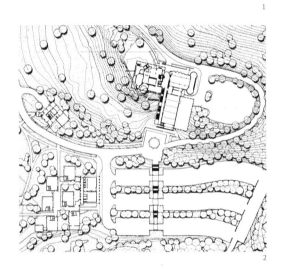

2

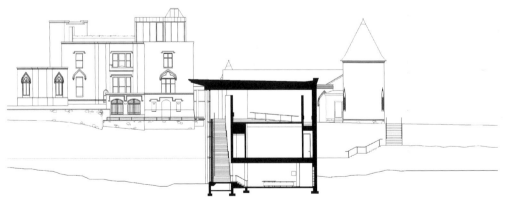

3

4

4

5

6

7

# Kauffman Foundation Headquarters

KANSAS CITY, MISSOURI : 1995–99

The Kauffman Foundation Headquarters occupies 37 acres of floodplain reconfigured into a network of ponds, wetlands, and waterfalls for controlling storm runoff. Into this setting the architects placed two long low office wings that fan out from a central lobby and offer expansive views of courtyards, gardens, and a restored creek. The building's centerpiece is a "town square" containing a flexible meeting space surrounded by seminar rooms of various types and sizes, including a kiva-like space that underscores the archaeological theme of the site plan. The detailing is surprisingly spare and understated for KMW—drywall, maple millwork, wood slat screens, buff brick, rolled copper roofs—in keeping with the foundation's philanthropic objectives.

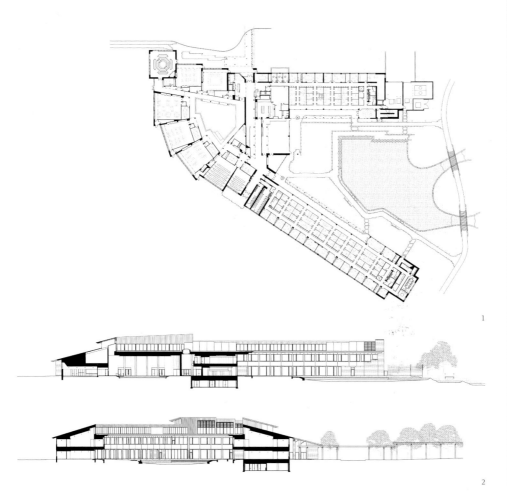

1

2      3

1: Courtyard and pond
2: View from courtyard
3: "Town Square"
4: Foyer and staircase
5: Wall detail

3

4

5

# Buildings and the Campus

College and university buildings account for two-thirds of Kallmann McKinnell & Wood's work, providing a well-bred alternative to the developer commissions they rarely get. Yet their approach to campus design is similar to their approach to cities. They try to balance formal expressiveness with respect for context; they fill in and add on; and they strive to connect fragments and complete patterns rather than create solitary monuments. This separates them from passionate formalists like Frank Gehry and Richard Meier, for whom a campus is essentially a tabula rasa for experimentation, an opportunity to shake things up. KMW's academic buildings are typically subtler and more tailored, reinforcing the sense of tradition and continuity that students expect, and for which alums are willing to donate generously. "They all want the campus to look like what they remember, or think they remember," says Michael McKinnell, underscoring the firm's basic strategy.

Satisfying this desire for continuity may involve little more than refreshing familiar details, as in the selective repetition of Victor Hornbostel motifs at the Goizueta School of Business at Emory University. Or it may require a careful reinterpretation of established patterns, as in Louis Marx Hall at Princeton University (**1**). Where it joins 1879 Hall it is properly quoined and finialed and symmetrical; at the opposite end, where it frames a campus courtyard and punctuates a key intersection with the city, it becomes crisp, spare, and asymmetrical. The transition is clear and unforced, yet with a sense of inevitability.

Harvard's Hauser Hall (**2**) represents a more complex form of mediation involving a beloved H.H. Richardson classroom building and the historically important—if not universally admired—Harkness Commons by Walter

Gropius. Hauser's brick façade and rusticated stone base, though flattened and abstracted, bow politely to Richardson's Austin Hall, while its curved backside and crisp steel and glass detailing speak the minimalist language of Gropius. Contextualism as fugue rather than applique. Even in campuses built from scratch, KMW attempts to make connections to history and local tradition. Singapore's National Institute of Education at Nanyang Technical University, opened in 2000, sits atop a low hill surrounded by a lush tropical landscape. The individual buildings, linked by continuous shaded arcades, all face a central courtyard, but the controlling metaphor of the plan is the ancient acropolis.

2

KMW's largest academic commission to date has been Washington University in St. Louis (3)—six buildings and a master plan over the last 15 years. With its Neo-gothic quads and broad lawns it presents a cinematically perfect image of a university. The architects played off this vernacular in their design of Simon Hall, home of the College of Business and Public Administration, by combining traditional ashlar stonework and fanciful gables—campus trademarks—with modern bay windows and a handsome interior courtyard that fills the building with natural light.

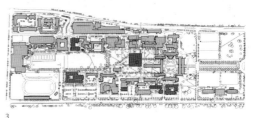
3

Yet at Washington University and elsewhere this disciplined balancing of old and new is being defeated by bloated programs that act like growth hormones on academic architecture. Directly across the great lawn from Simon Hall sits the Knight Center, housing the school's MBA and executive training programs. Although the forms and details are once again Neo-Gothic, the scale is closer to a hotel and conference center than a traditional college building. Even with skilled architects and good intentions, such problems are nearly insoluble.

# Shad Hall, Athletic Fitness Center, Harvard Business School

BOSTON, MASSACHUSETTS : 1985–89

Shad Hall, while modern in plan and section, works hard to blend with its surroundings. Red brick, green trim, and pitched slate roofs are staples of the Harvard vernacular, along with white mullioned windows and ivy covered walls. The south side of Shad bulks up in response to Harvard Stadium, while on the north it adjusts to the residential scale of the Business School dormitories.

The interiors are thoroughly contemporary, with a gymnasium, jogging track, and squash and racquetball courts all arranged around a central atrium that brings natural light to all levels of the building. There's also a pub and restaurant for slackers. Materials range from polished concrete and exposed steel to textured plaster and oak flooring, producing a stylish hybrid that combines old and new, tradition and invention.

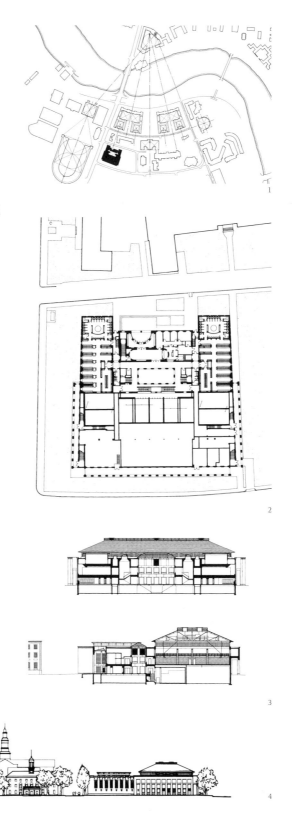

1: Site plan
2: The splayed walls of the plan
   follow the radial geometry
   of the campus south of the
   Charles River.
3: Sections
4: Elevation on Harvard Street
5: Southwest corner

1: Entrance façade
2: View from south
3: Arcade on Harvard Street
4: Entrance forecourt and column
5: Pub
6: Gymnasium and running track
7: Atrium connecting all levels
8: Grand stair linking atrium to
   squash courts

4

5

6

7

8

# Nancy Lee and Perry R. Bass Center for Molecular and Structural Biology, Yale University

NEW HAVEN, CONNECTICUT : 1987–93

The Bass Center at Yale is a creative synthesis in both architectural and academic terms. It closes the northern end of an important university quadrangle containing Philip Johnson's Kline Tower as well as neo-Gothic and modern science buildings. The tower's covered walkway provides a key organizing element, while the use of brick, brownstone, steel, and glass reflect the amalgam of historical and contemporary styles of both the quad and the rest of the campus. A dramatic staircase leads from Whitney Avenue to the main entrance on the courtyard level. The Bass Center houses the department of molecular and structural biology, itself a hybrid produced by the graying of traditional boundaries between scientific disciplines. The plan reflects this new reality, with offices and laboratories on opposite sides of a long interior street that connects to adjacent buildings by turrets and an arched bridge. The offices face the courtyard, the labs the campus's northern extension.

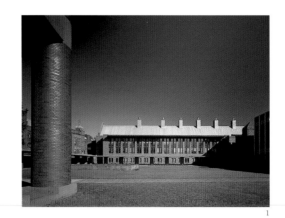

1

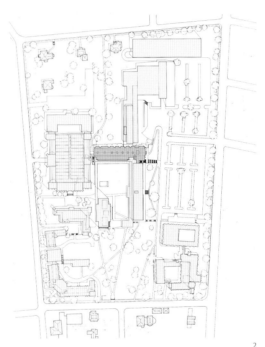

2

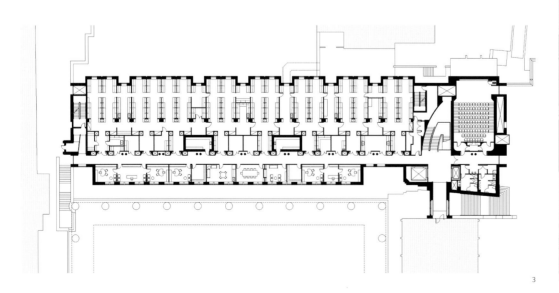

3      4

1: The center completes an
   important quadrangle
2: Site plan
3: Floor plan
4: North façade of laboratories
   and Kline Tower

5

6

7

8

# Hauser Hall,
# Harvard Law School

CAMBRIDGE, MASSACHUSETTS : 1991–94

Hauser Hall, a five-story classroom and faculty office building, sits on the north edge of Holmes Field, a large grassy rectangle between Harvard's Law School and its main biology and chemistry buildings. The foursquare brick and stone front responds to the geometry of the field and its grid of trees, while the muscular entry arch and rusticated base acknowledge H.H. Richardson's Austin Hall a few doors away. In back, however, Hauser's bold curve swells out towards Walter Gropius's Harkness Commons, pulling it and its sunken trapezoidal courtyard into the larger composition. In this way it serves as both wall and door, marking the boundary of Holmes Field but also allowing space to escape around the corners in search of Gropius. This interplay between old and new, assertion and reticence, is underscored by the building materials: brick and limestone to recall the historic Yard, steel and glass and precise metal trim to express the present.

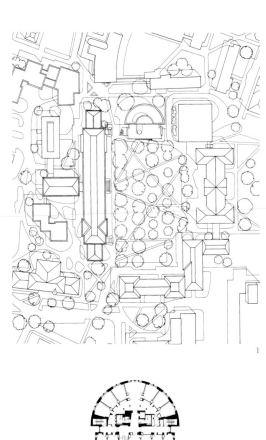

1

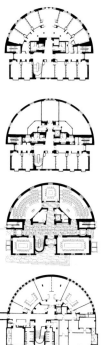

2

3

4

1: Site plan
2: Floor plans
3: Section through Hauser
   Hall and elevation
   of Langdell Library
4: South façade

1: View from Holmes Field
2: Faculty office bay windows
3: West entrance and exedra
4: View from Harkness Common
5: Wall detail
6: Volume study

4

6

5

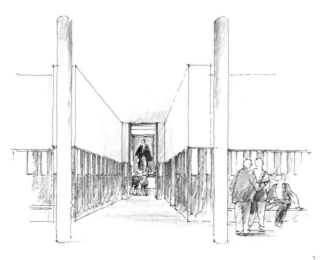

4

5

6

# Marx Hall,
# Princeton University

PRINCETON, NEW JERSEY : 1990–94

This modest 16,000-square-foot addition to
Princeton's Philosophy Department could be a
short course in sensitive contextualism. It begins
at 1879 Hall, the department's historic home, and
ends as a small gabled tower of offices and classrooms, slightly rotated, that marks the entrance
to McCosh Walk, an important campus gateway.
In between, the architects carefully integrated
old and new: gables, bay windows, and red brick,
but also large modern windows framed in thin
steel strips. The extension includes classrooms,
faculty offices, and a library, along with a lesson
in how to add on without taking over.

3

1

2

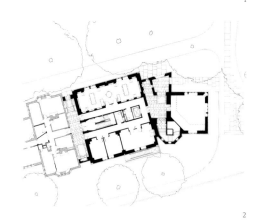

4

5   6

# Miller Performing Arts Center, Alfred University

ALFRED, NEW YORK : 1991–94

The new performing arts center at Alfred University, named for the founder of Arrow International, possesses the same minimalist elegance as the corporate headquarters: large expanses of handsomely detailed red brick, crisp but varied window openings, a flexible plan that capitalizes on variations in topography and elevation. From the street, visitors can catch glimpses of rehearsal rooms as well as the costume and design shops. Behind and below, where the site falls away towards woods and playing fields, are the main performance spaces, including a 250-seat theater, an acting and directing rehearsal hall, and a dance studio with a 28-foot ceiling and spectacular views of the valley.

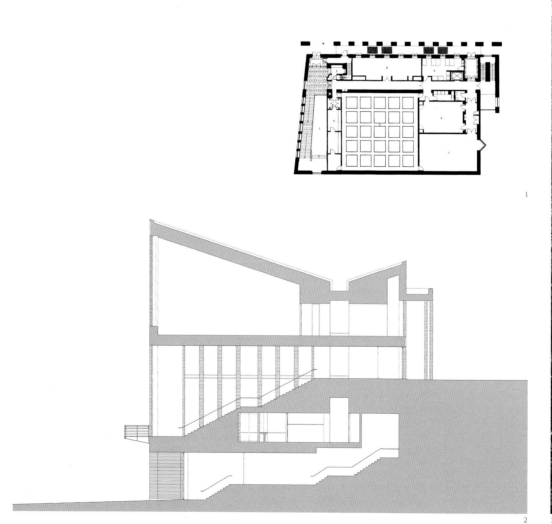

1

2    3

1: Floor plan
2: Section
3: East elevation with windows
   lighting stair hall

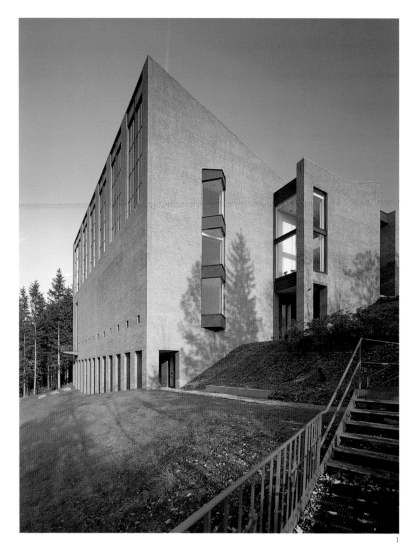

1: Northwest corner
2: Street front and
   student entrance
3: North façade
4: Night view of north façade
5: Rehearsal space
6: Corner window
7: Theater

5

6

7

# Goizueta School of Business, Emory University

ATLANTA, GEORGIA : 1991–97

The Goizueta School of Business at Emory University is a five-story U shape that turns a confident face to a busy urban intersection. The building is organized hierarchically, with the main public spaces (classrooms, cafeteria, student lounges) on the lower floors and faculty offices and conference rooms above. The public floors open onto a loggia that connects to an outdoor amphitheater where students gather between classes and for graduation. One of KMW's signature circular staircases anchors the core of the building, providing both an architectural focus and sense of occasion. The detailing of the façade and arcades recalls the original Victor Hornbostel buildings on campus.

1

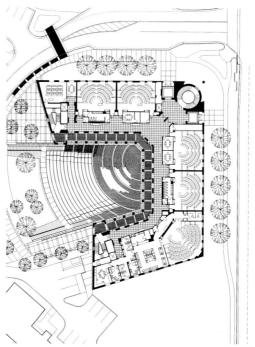

2

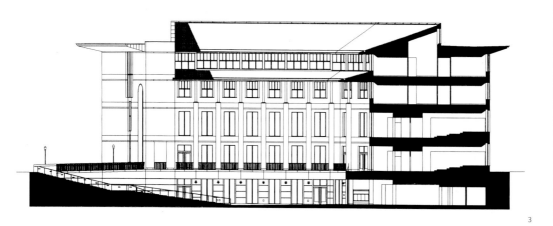

3

4

1: Campus site plan
2: Floor plan
3: Section
4: Courtyard

1: West façade and courtyard
2: Entrance façade
3, 4: Colonnade around courtyard
5: Amphitheater terrace
6: Corner staircase
7: Student alcove looking out
   on courtyard

4

5

6

7

# Young Library,
# University of Kentucky

LEXINGTON, KENTUCKY : 1992–98

The Young Library is the centerpiece of a major campus extension, and therefore considerably flashier stylistically than most recent KMW designs. Each façade features a brick and stone arcade surmounted by lofty porticos extending the full height of the building. Sets of tall branching columns support signature overhanging roofs. The building, Palladian in volume and of bi-axial symmetry, is organized around a sky-lit court and central rotunda with book stacks, study areas, and tall loggias on all four sides. An asymmetrically placed grand staircase leads to the main floor and the central reading room above.

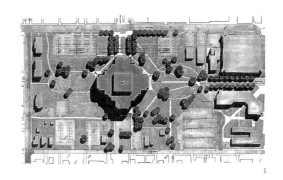

1

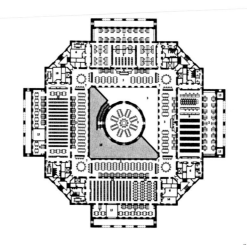

2

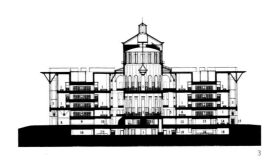

3

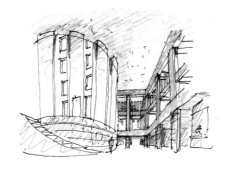

1: Site plan
2: Main floor plan
3: Section
4: Sketch of atrium
5: Perimeter loggias overlook
   the campus on all sides.

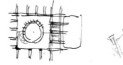

4          5

1

2

3

4

1

2

3

4

5

# Max Fisher College of Business, The Ohio State University

COLUMBUS, OHIO : 1993–99

The Max Fisher school of business is a group of six masonry buildings on the northern edge of the Ohio State Campus, of which KMW designed three: Gerlach Hall, a 3-story, 69,000-square-foot building containing classrooms, administrative offices, and recreational space for the school's graduate management program; Schoenbaum Hall, the center for the undergraduate program that includes 14 class-rooms and a 300-seat auditorium; Mason Hall, the school's main library and research center Each has its own distinguishing architectural feature—portico, rotunda, street façade. KMW's three buildings, arranged around an open-ended courtyard, are unified by consistent cornice heights, continuous arcades and a shared palette of materials that includes brick and granite.

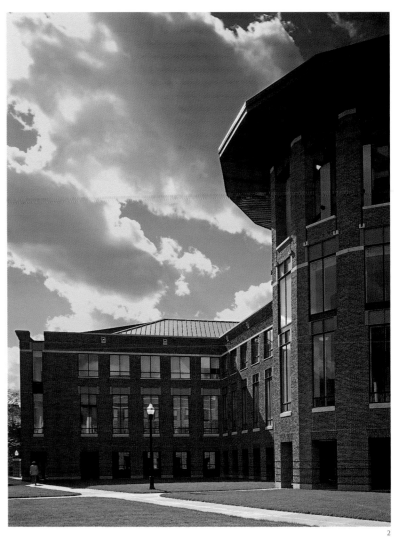

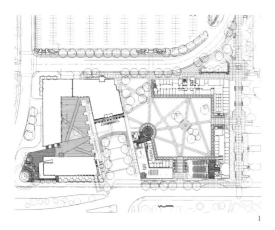

1: Site plan of quadrangles
2: The rotunda of Mason Hall
3: Student lounge, Gerlach Hall
4: Columnar façade of the lounge
5: View through east portal
   of courtyard

5

# Academic Buildings and Master Plan, Washington University

ST. LOUIS, MISSOURI : 1982–2001

KMW has been working at Washington University since the mid-1980s, producing a campus master plan and six buildings, including a plant conservatory, a school of business and public administration, and several restorations and additions.

Their strategy has been to work within the guidelines of the original 1899 master plan by Cope and Stewardson, which used loosely linked bar buildings to create informal quadrangles reminiscent of English prototypes. The business school, Simon Hall, and the Knight Executive Education Center are both organized this way, with the central courtyards providing congenial gathering places for students and faculty. This arrangement also tempers the spatial impact of dramatically expanded academic programs, which are skewing the scale of many American campuses. The architectural language of the KMW buildings is a contemporary interpretation of the school's Gothic Revival vernacular, combining portals, gables, and rough ashlar stonework with contemporary double-height bay windows and precise metal trim.

1

2

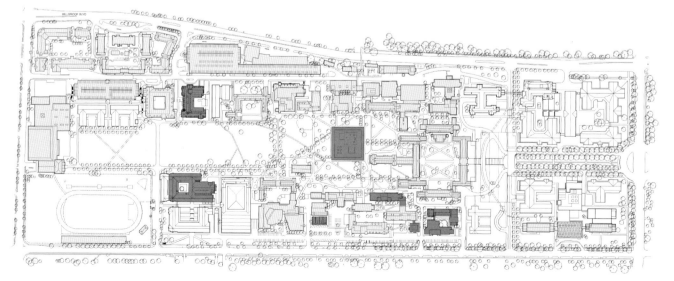

3

1: Concept sketches of
   Simon Hall
2: Cope and Stewardson
   block plan of 1889
3: Final extended master plan
   in association with Mackey
   Mitchell Associates, with
   existing buildings in light
   grey and KMW buildings in
   dark grey.

4: Main lawn with Simon Hall
   in foreground
5: Simon Hall plan
6: Knight Executive Center plan
7: Aerial view of Simon Hall
8, 9: View of Simon Hall from
   green, and entrance façade

4

5

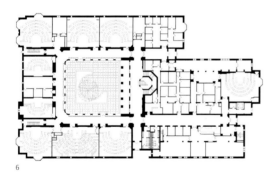

6

7

8

9

1: Simon Hall courtyard
2: Plant growth facility 1985 in association with Gilmore Malcic & Canon
3: James McDonnell Hall 1987
4, 5: Knight Center's oval staircase and dining hall
6: W. Brown School of Social Work hall restoration 1993

7: The Charles Knight Executive Education Center courtyard
8: The Olin Library addition and renovation (completion 2004)

# Yale Law School Renovation

NEW HAVEN, CONNECTICUT : 1987–2000

Designed and constructed in phases over a thirteen-year period, KMW's renovations substantially upgraded James Gamble Rogers' distinguished 1930's Collegiate Gothic building for the Yale Law School. Beyond the total replacement of the systems infrastructure and the complete rehabilitation of the exterior envelope, the project rejuvenated offices, classrooms, and student social spaces, including the transformation of a dormitory wing into an administrative and faculty center. The law library, which occupies six levels, was the core of the renovation effort. Here KMW juxtaposed the extension of the existing materials palette of oak, stone, and plaster with modern interventions in section, bringing daylight and spatial connections to previously inboard, hermetic interiors.

1

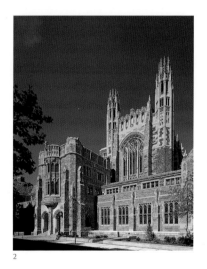

2

3

4

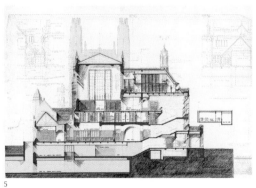

5

6

7

# National Institue of Education, Nanyang Technological University

SINGAPORE : 1992–2001

The Institute is a village of academic buildings enclosing a long triangular green. The schools of Education, Arts, Sciences, and Physical Education all face this central space, their similar façades creating a continuous horizontal sequence of arcades. The three academic levels, mostly flexible clear-span spaces, are connected by exterior staircases and protected from the intense heat by louvers and deep overhangs. The green is closed at one end by the administration building and at the other by a U-shaped library, with smaller buildings for theater, art, and physical education sprinkled between. Expansion will be accommodated by extending the wings of the existing buildings and adding more specialized structures similar to the art gallery and theater.

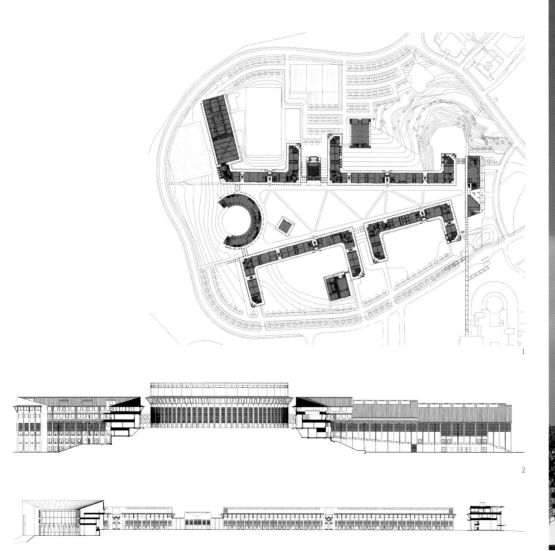

1

2

3    4

4

5

6

7

8

# Epilogue

BY ROBERT CAMPBELL

Both Gerhard Kallmann and Michael McKinnell came to the United States from Britain. Perhaps it's appropriate, therefore, to begin with a quote from the eminent British critic J. M. Richards, whose words are among the sanest and wisest I know:

*"Architecture cannot progress by the fits and starts that a succession of revolutionary ideas involves. Nor, if it exists perpetually in a state of revolution, will it achieve any kind of public following, since public interest thrives on a capacity to admire what is already familiar and a need to label and classify."*

Or to cite another ex-Brit, the historian Kenneth Frampton:

*"Now once again we live in an age in which speed and cybernetic disposability are advanced as the order of the day. But it must be seriously questioned whether speed and ephemerality ever had anything to do with architecture, and further, whether architecture is not, to the contrary, an essentially anachronistic form of art, whose fundamental task is to stand against the fungibility of things and the mortality of the species."*

Both Frampton and Richards argue in favor of continuity in the history of architecture, as opposed to exciting revolutions of taste every few years. The career of the partnership of Kallmann McKinnell & Wood, as it has developed over time, has become an embodiment of ideas like those of Frampton and Richards. KMW belong to what one might call the middle tradition of modern architecture. They certainly do not progress by the fits and starts of revolutionary ideas. But at the same time, they do not seek merely to please the public with sentimental replays of the beloved styles of the past. As Michael McKinnell has said, they seek to position themselves between memory and invention, drawing energy from both.

The 20th century was an age obsessed with invention. In architecture, heroic figures like Walter Gropius, Mies van der Rohe, Le Corbusier, Frank Gehry, and others pioneered what was seen as the brave path of modernism. But there is another, less confrontational tradition of modern architecture. It encompasses, let us say, such figures as Otto Wagner, Adolf Loos, and Josef Hoffmann in Vienna, Frank Lloyd Wright, Bernard Maybeck, Eliel Saarinen, and Louis Kahn in the United States, Alvar Aalto in Finland, Carlo Scarpa in Italy, and numerous others. It is to this group that KMW belong.

These were architects who chose a middle path between tradition and innovation. They preferred not to lose touch with the conventional language of architectural form, as that language developed through history and as it is understood by the general public. But they reached forward to invent when it was appropriate to do so: to accommodate and express changes in the ways people live, or changes in culture and its esthetic, or changes in the technology of building. The work of such architects lives in the tension between the present and the past—between McKinnell's "memory and invention." Maybe tension isn't the right word. It lives in the way the building maintains a conversation with the past while addressing the needs of the present and the future.

Architectural traditionalists and architectural avant-gardists appear to be opposites. But in truth they are more like each other than they are different. They share a desire to shove aside the present, and to replace it with a Utopia of another age. Reactionaries seek a Utopia of the past. Avant-gardists seek a Utopia of the future. Both Utopias are simplified fictions. It's much easier to design a Utopia for another, largely imaginary age than it is to confront the complexities of the present. KMW, by contrast, operate in the present. They understand that the present can only be understood—that it can only exist, really—by reference to both the past and the future. Janus-like, their buildings look both ways.

My connection with KMW is now a long one. Michael was my principal thesis advisor when I was an architecture student at the Harvard Graduate School of Design. A dozen years later, I was a consultant to the American Academy of Arts and Sciences during the time when KMW were designing and building the Academy's new headquarters in Cambridge. During that dozen years, the work of the partners changed radically.

KMW, as is well known, first came to attention in 1962 as the winners of a national design competition for a new Boston City Hall. At the time, both were teaching in New York at the Columbia University School of Architecture. Neither had ever designed and built a building in his own name.

City Hall is very much a child of the late work of Le Corbusier, most obviously his great monastery of La Tourette in France. Corbu in his late years became fascinated by the expressive power of raw poured concrete, as he had witnessed it in the massive fortifications of World War II. At the same time, English architects, under the influence of socialist ideals, sought a kind of architecture that would be as gritty and honest as the working class itself. The result was the style that came to be called, for reasons never entirely clear, Brutalism. Boston City Hall is by far the most significant example of Brutalism in the United States. It was, in its day, very much an avant-garde design.

I think it is fair to say that in City Hall, KMW created a building whose sources lay in the private subculture of modernist architecture, a culture that even today is little appreciated by the general public. Members of the public tend to regard it as aggressive and intimidating, isolated from its surroundings in its vast plaza, and lacking the texture, color, and detail that invite one to move closer to a building.

But City Hall is a building of enormous presence. Its power comes from its seeming somehow to have survived and endured. In time, it may well become one of those treasured icons that we view with a mixture of affection and exasperation, a building that is great without being beautiful. It's best thought of as a kind of civic castle, still slightly grim as it awaits the arrival of the festivities and memorabilia that will make it into a living history. As McKinnell once said in an interview, "The building was conceived as an armature, a framework, which would be, we hoped, invested by subsequent generations of Bostonians with their own marks and their own decoration and their own embellishment."

What's interesting is that even in this early building, KMW were drawing from a rich multiplicity of sources, were already in dialogue with many pasts. The floor plan, to cite one example, is very unlike anything Corbu would have done, but instead is clearly modeled on the plans of ancient Mycenaean palaces such as Knossos. Already in this early work we see the emergence of the essential KMW: architects of the metaphorical and the narrative.

After City Hall, KMW designed other good buildings in a similar manner, notably the gym at Exeter and the Boston Five Cents Savings Bank. Then bold concrete architecture began to go out of fashion. KMW responded by developing what became its mature manner. The turn-around began with the American Academy of Arts and Sciences in Cambridge.

Forgive a personal recollection. After being selected as the architect for this building, Kallmann and McKinnell were invited to dinner at a Cambridge restaurant. Present were the president and director of the Academy and the Academy's architectural advisor, Lawrence Anderson, former dean of the school of architecture and planning at MIT. Andy had written the superb program for the building, which stated that "the Academy does not want to become the vehicle for a personal or trendy stylistic statement." Nor, he wrote, should its building be recognizably the product of any single moment in architectural history. He was entrusted with the mission of enunciating the sole caveat the Academy wished to impose on its architects. After a pleasant dinner, he did so.

"There will be one rule," Andy announced. "No exposed concrete indoors or out." Kallmann paused barely a nanosecond before replying, "We never would have considered it."

The Academy design was the first in what became the KMW tradition of buildings that occupy a middle ground between the traditional and the innovative. While it was being designed, one could see many books about architects of the past lying open in the office. I remember Alvar Aalto, Greene and Greene, Louis Kahn, Charles Rennie Mackintosh, Charles Voysey, and Mark Girouard's *Sweetness and Light*, a study of late Victorian architecture. Hoffmann and Wright are other strong influences, and Carlo Scarpa, who died during the design phase, is silently memorialized in the shape of the Academy's fireplaces. But sources were limitless. They included, or so I believe, a converted barn in Lincoln, Massachusetts, a painted ceiling at the Boston Museum of Fine Arts, and a now-demolished athletic building at Harvard. And the Academy's floor plan, like that of the very different City Hall, recalls that of Knossos: a regular orthogonal order at the center which then grows more ragged as it moves out to engage the surrounding landscape. In KMW's work, such sources are never replicated literally. They are fully digested, and they typically re-emerge in a slightly abstracted form, often as if we were seeing a light sketch of the original. Rich in allusions, the KMW building becomes, like a good poem, an object of fascination you can never quite get to the bottom of.

At the Academy, too, KMW deliberately worked to evoke a sense of the passage of time. As with some works by Aalto, the landscape seems to be chewing into the building at one corner, hinting of its eventual dissolution and death. Time-sensitive, too, is the fact that many of the design motifs recall the Edwardian era of the early 20th century, a great period when architecture was poised between a dying Victorian tradition and an oncoming modernist revolution.

McKinnell has written eloquently of what he calls "re-presentation" in architecture. By this he means the ways in which a building does not literally embody, but rather re-presents certain themes. It may, for example, re-present the means of its construction. Literal construction today is usually hidden; the Academy, for example, is structurally supported by an invisible steel frame. The facts of construction are instead re-presented in the brick piers (some of which are rhetorical, holding up nothing) and wood brackets of the finished building. A story is told about construction, rather than construction being literally expressed. Also re-presented in the Academy is the landscape. The building becomes an abstracted, geometricized extension of the knoll on which it stands. Re-presented, too, are iconic myths of the origins of architecture and of shelter itself, as the architects' sketches remind us: the tree house, the column as surrogate human figure, the primitive hut, the rural villa.

I've paid so much attention to the American Academy because it's the KMW building I know best, and because it was in so many ways the turning point of the firm's career. KMW went on to explore many of the Academy's motifs in other superb buildings, notably the Becton Dickinson and Arrow headquarters buildings. In Boston, KMW became, in some degree, the successor to Charles Follen McKim as the city's official designer of civic and cultural buildings. Among these are Boston City Hall, Government Center Garage, the Boston Five Cents Savings Bank (now Borders Books), Back Bay Station, the superb Hynes Convention Center; and at Harvard the Shad Hall Athletic Fitness Center and Hauser Hall at the law school.

University work has become, in recent years, the largest part of KMW's portfolio. It's the kind of work that fits the aspirations of these architects. Any university is a city in miniature. It offers the architect a chance to deal imaginatively with issues of memory and of community in a relatively controlled setting. McKinnell has said that "universities represent, for most people, the time in their lives when they were most conscious of their physical surroundings, and the time when they lived in an environment that referred to the past....There's a yearning for a sense of continuity, for stasis and permanence, an environment that links us to the past."

That is the paradox of a university. It has two quite contradictory missions. It must hoard the wisdom of the past, in its libraries and in the memories of its scholars, and it must invent the future, in its laboratories and in the brains of its creative thinkers. With their interest in an architecture that connects both back and forward, KMW have proved to be ideal designers for American college campuses.

Perhaps the 21st century will be less obsessed with arbitrary invention and more inclined to perceive new buildings as further chapters in an ongoing discourse of architecture, treating the past—all of the past—with respect, while innovating freely and confidently to address new circumstances. If so, there is hope that architecture will remain ever fresh and ever familiar at the same time.

In thinking about these issues, I'm always reminded of the great line by Robert Frost, who said that for him, writing free verse would be like playing tennis without a net. Without a net, a court, and a book of rules, how could he tell when he'd made a good shot? Architecture, like every art, requires a set of conventions against which new work can be measured. There can be no such thing as originality in the absence of conventions. How can you be unconventional without conventions?

In the work of Kallmann McKinnell & Wood, there is an understanding that a language (or perhaps languages) of architecture does exist, and that for the wise and literate architect, there is no greater source of richness and meaning than the game of setting memory and invention in play with each other.

# Chronology

Boston City Hall and Plaza 1962–68, Boston, MA
Kallmann McKinnell & Knowles in joint venture with
Campbell & Aldrich and Le Messurier Associates

Government Center Garage 1964–1970, Boston, MA
In joint venture with Samuel Glazer & Partners

Phillips Exeter Academy, Athletics Facility 1965–1970
Exeter, NH

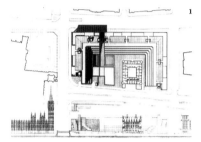

Parliamentary Office Building Competition 1971
London, England
In joint venture with D&M Craig, London

Boston Five Cents Savings Bank 1966–1972
Boston, MA

Roosevelt Island Motorgate 1970–1975
New York, NY

Dudley Street Library 1967–1976
Roxbury, MA

Woodhull Hospital, 1969–1978
Brooklyn, NY
In joint venture with Russo & Sonder, NY

American Academy of Arts & Sciences 1977–1981
Cambridge, MA

Daresco Commercial Center Project 1981
Damman, Saudi Arabia
In joint venture with Khudary & Uthman Int.

Aspen Performing Arts Center Project 1983
Aspen, CO

Back Bay Station, 1976–1987
Boston, MA
In joint venture with Bond Ryder Associates

Becton Dickinson & Company Corporate &
Division HQ 1981–1992,Franklin Lakes, NJ

Academic Buildings, Washington University in St.
Louis 1982–2002, Masterplan in Association with
Mackey Mitchell Associates

Hynes Veterans Memorial Convention Center
1983–1988, Boston, MA

Columbia University Law School Expansion Project
1984, New York, NY

U.S. Embassy and Chancery 1983–1988
Dhaka, Bangladesh

Asian Export Art Wing–Peabody Essex Museum
1984–1988, Salem, MA

The Pier 4 Development Project 1986–1987
Boston, MA.

Shad Hall Athletic Fitness Center 1985–1989
Harvard Business School, Boston, MA

Paul J. Kellner Performing Arts Center 1985–1991
Milton Academy, Milton, MA

Newton Free Library 1986 - 1991
Newton, MA
In joint venture with Tappé & Associates

Arrow International Corporate Headquarters
1989–1991, Reading, PA

Bass Center for Molecular & Structural Biology
1987–1993, Yale University, New Haven, CT

Getty Museum - Invited Competition 1993
Malibu, CA

Posner Hall, Grad. School of Industrial Administration
1989–1993, Carnegie Mellon University
Pittsburgh, PA

Hauser Hall, Harvard Law School 1991–1994
Harvard University, Cambridge, MA

Louis J. Marx '53 Hall, Center for Human Values
1990–1994, Princeton University, Princeton, NJ

Miller Performing Arts Center 1991–1995
Alfred University, Alfred, NY

U.S. Embassy - Invited Competition Project 1995
Berlin, Germany

U.S. Embassy - Invited Competition Project 1995
Berlin, Germany

Center for Electrical Engineering 1989–1997
University of Washington, Seattle, WA

Seafirst Executive Education Center 1990–1997
University of Washington, Seattle, WA

Roberto C. Goizueta School of Business  1991–1997
Emory, University, Atlanta, GA
In association with Taylor Anderson Architects Inc.

Private residence 1993–1997
Berks County, PA

DeCordova Museum - Renovation and New Wing
1992–1998, Lincoln, MA

William T. Young Commonwealth Library 1992–1998
University of Kentucky, Lexington, KY

Yale Law School - Renovation and Expansion
1987–2000, Yale University, New Haven, CT

Organisation for the Prohibition of Chemical Weapons
World HQ 1993–1998,The Hague, The Netherlands,
In association with Kuiper-Oosterheert-
Wubben Architects

Edward W. Brooke Courthouse 1993–1999
Boston, MA

Max M. Fisher College of Business 1993–1999
The Ohio State University, Columbus, OH
In association with Karlsberger Architecture Inc.

Ewing Marion Kauffman Foundation Headquarters
1995–2001, Kansas City, MO

James. H. Quillen U.S. Federal Courthouse
1995–2001, Greeneville, TN
In joint venture with Hnedak Bobo Group

National Institute of Education Master Plan
1992–2000, Nanyang Technological University,
Singapore, In association with PWD Consultants

Harvey W. Wiley Federal Building 1995 - 2000
U.S. Food and Drug Administration, College Park, MD
In association with HDR Architects Inc.

Walters Art Museum - Renovation 1996–2001
Baltimore, MD

Biomedical Engineering and Med. Science Building
1997–2001, University of Virginia, Charlottesville, VA,
In association with HDR Architects Inc.

Law Library, 1997–2001
Howard University, Washington, DC
In joint venture with Baker Cooper Architects

Chamberlain Residence Hall and Dining Hall
1998–2001Bowdoin College, Brunswick, ME

Loudoun County Courts Complex - Expansion &
Renovation 1997–2001, Leesburg, VA
In association with HDR Architects Inc.

Carl B. Stokes Federal Courthouse and Offices
1994–2002, Cleveland, OH
In joint venture with Karlsberger Companies

Independence Visitors' Center 1998–2003
Philadelphia, PA

World Trade Center West 1998–2003
Boston, MA.

GSA Federal Laboratories 1998–2003
Beltsville, MD

Fairfax County Courthouse 1999–2003
Fairfax, VA
In association with HDR Architecture Inc.

Physical Sciences 1 2000–2004
University of California, Riverside California

Student Center 1997–2004
University of Massachusetts, Boston, MA

Jack S. Blanton Museum of Art 2001–2005
University of Texas, Austin, TX
In association with Booziotis Company

Mecklenburg County Courthouse 2003–2006
Charlotte, NC, In joint venture with Schenkel Schultz
Architecture and HDR Arch. Inc.

# Awards & Honors

**Firm Recognition**

1984 American Institute of Architects,
   AIA Firm of the Year Award

1987 Louis Sullivan Award for Architecture

1994 Boston Society of Architects Firm Honor Award

**Boston City Hall**

1969 AIA Honor Award for Excellence in Architectural Design

1970 Harleston Parker Medal, BSA/City of Boston

**Boston Five Cents Savings Bank**

1975 Harleston Parker Medal, BSA/City of Boston

**American Academy of Arts and Sciences**

1980 BSA Export Award, Highest Honor

1982 AIA Honor Award for Excellence in Architectural Design

1983 Harleston Parker Medal, BSA/City of Boston

**Back Bay Station, Massachusetts Bay Transit Authority**

1987 Design Award, New England Masonry Association

**John B. Hynes Veterans Memorial Convention Center**

1989 Harleston Parker Medal, BSA/City of Boston

1991 BSA Honor Award for Architecture

1991 BSA Honor Award for Interiors

1993 AIA Honor Award for Excellence in Architectural Design

**Becton Dickinson & Company Corporate Headquarters**

1988 BSA Export Award, Highest Honor

1990 AIA Honor Award for Excellence in Architectural Design

1990 BSA Honor Award for Architecture

**Asian Export Art Wing, Peabody Essex Museum**

1991 BSA Export Award, Highest Honor

1991 BSA Interior Architecture Award

**Newton Free Library**

1994 AIA New England Honor Award for Architecture

**Shad Hall Athletic Center, Harvard Business School**

1994 Harleston Parker Medal, BSA/City of Boston

**Becton Dickinson & Company Divisional Headquarters**

1994 BSA Honor Award for Architecture

1998 AIA Honor Award for Excellence in Architectural Design

**Hauser Hall, Harvard Law School**

1994 Harleston Parker Medal, BSA/City of Boston

1994 BSA Award for Design Excellence

1997 AIA Brick In Architecture Award

**Princeton University, Louis Marx, Jr. '53 Hall,
Center for Human Values**

1996 BSA Honor Award for Architecture

1999 AIA Brick In Architecture Award

**Yale University, Bass Center for Molecular &
Structural Biology**

1997 AIA Honor Award for Excellence in Architectural Design

1997 AIA Brick In Architecture Award

**Arrow International Corporate Headquarters**

1994 AIA Honor Award for Excellence in Interior Design

1995 AIA Honor Award for Excellence in Architectural Design

1998 BSA Honor Award for Architecture

**Bowdoin College, Chamberlain Residence Hall**

1999 BSA/AIA Honor Award for Design Excellence in Housing

**Alfred University, Miller Performing Arts Center**

1999 BSA Honor Award for Architecture

**Edward W. Brooke Courthouse**

2002 BSA Honor Award for Architecture

**Harvey W. Wiley Federal Building,
United States Food & Drug Administration**

2002 GSA Federal Design Award

**Carl B. Stokes United States Courthouse**

2002 American Architecture Award, The Chicago Athenaeum

**DeCordova Museum & Sculpture Park**

2003 BSA Honor Award for Architecture

**Yale Law School Renovation**

2003 BSA Honor Award for Architecture

# Associates and Collaborators

**PRINCIPALS**
Gerhard M. Kallmann
N. Michael McKinnell
Henry A. Wood
S. Fiske Crowell, Jr.
Hans Huber
Rayford Law
Bruno Pfister
Theodore Szostkowski
Bruce A. Wood

**ASSOCIATE PRINCIPALS**
Kathryn MacKenzie
Stephanie Mallis

**SENIOR ASSOCIATES**
Mark DeShong
Don Klema
Ronald Steffek
Gary Tondorf-Dick

**ASSOCIATES**
Peter Bacot
Alicia Crothers
Martin Dermady
Donald Eurich
Timothy Scarlett
Anne Tansantisuk

**COLLABORATORS**
Robert Abrahamson
Andrea Adams
Nancy Adelson
Jennifer Allen
Kainja Allen
Thomas Allen
Saif Alsayed
Edward Alshut
Susan Amirkhan
Beatrice Ammann
Ruben Anderegg
Kristin Andres
Ato Apiafi
Frank Armentano
Blake Auchincloss
Claudia Bancalari
Ronald Barber
Joyce Bariamis
Alexandra Barker
William Barry
Jeffrey Bartsch
Heidi Beebe
Shirley Bender
Edward Benner
Ralph Bennett
Ruth Bennett
Peter Benoit
Debra Berger
Susan Berger-Jones
Jack Bialosky
Lawrence Birch
Stephan Birk
Michael Bischoff
Brian Black
Alexandra Blei
James Blount
Peter Boehm
Kimberly Bolduc
Rosa Bolet
Allen Bomer
Kathleen Bond
Aaron Booth
Billy Gene Born
Ann Marie Borys

Tricia Bowman
Earl Branting
Anna Brigham
Dewitt Brock
Jeffrey Brown
Anka Buch
William Buckingham
Peter Bucklin
Steven Bull
Theodore Burton
Peter Butenschon
Peter Byrne
Laura Cabo
Niall Cain
Jacqueline Camenisch
Richard Campaman
Roger Cardinal
Edward Carfagno
Charles Carlin
Ginette Castro
John Catlin
Michael Chagnon
Kenneka Chambers
Pamela Chang
Szu-Wen Chang
Dan Chen
Kuen-Feng Chen
Michael Chervenak
Peter Choi
Shih-I Chou
Elaine Chow
Nancy Clapp
Scott Clinton
Amy Coburn
John Coburn
Alice Coggins
Christopher Collier
Deborah Collins
Patrick Cooleyback
Peter Coombie
Kenneth Cooper
William Cope
Vincent Cortina
Barbara Cote
Jonathan Craig
Angus Crowe
Peter Crowley
Terry Crystal
Marsha Cuddeback
Steven Dadagian
Christian Dagg
Ahmed Darwish
Dominac Daveta
Andrew Davis
William Dawson
David De Celis
Jeffrey Delvy
Michael Dembowski
Stephen Dermargousiam
Madhukar Deshmukh
Paul Desjardins
Shaohua Di
James Dodge
Paul Dodge
Douglas Doleza
Timothy Donahue
Gerard Dopp
Aidan Doyle
Jeff Dreyfus
Pamela Drondorff
Lloyd Dyson
Kelli Eagan
Valeria Earl
Steven Ehlbeck

Robert Elfer
Mathew Ellsworth
Brain Ely
Robert Enlow
Donnelley Erdman
Gail Ernst
Chun-Kai Fang
Barbara Farina
Patricia Farrell
Rachel Feinstein
Nadia Felix
Thomas Fels
Karl Fender
Joshua Fenollosa
Carla Fernandez
Ileana Fernandez
Debra Fesak
David Feth
Eric Figueroa
Andy Filmore
George Fisher
Julie Fisher
Blythe Forcey
Marc Ford
Robin Ford
Melanie Francis
Paul Frazier
Hannelore Freer
Sam Garcia
Gary Gardner
Richard Garfield
John Garrahan
Russell Gerard
Shauna Gillies-Smith
Jonathan Ginnis
Susan Gist
Barbara Giurlando
Christina Golen
Antonio Gomes
Aimee Goodwin
Dianne Gorman
Ramsay Gourd
Karen Grabau
Ann-Charlotte Green
Donald Grinberg
Heather Groff
Amy Hahn
Nathaniel Hailey
Abdul Halim
Michael Hall
Robin Hancock
Charlotte Hanks
Robert Hannisian
Carolyn Hansen
John Harden
Sara Harper
Kenneth Hartfiel
Meghan Harty
Bruce Harvey
Ann Haxton
John Hayes
Christopher Hays
Maarten Henkes
James Herold
Emily Hertz
Lai Sin Hew
Jason Hickey
Eric Hill
John Hillman
Patrick Hislop
Ed Hodges
Lillian Hodges
Heather Hoeksema
Jeff Holmes

Mark Homburg
Andrea Homolac
Lynn Hopkins
Marjorie Houk
Jeffrey Huang
Mazie Huh
Graham Hunter
Jayne Huxtable
Alison Induni
Chi Keung Ip
Noa Isaacson
Anthony Jackson
Rick Jackson
Elizabeth Jacques
Thomas Jin
Bradley Johnson
Constanze Joussen
Michael Kaonohi
Henry Keating
Mark Keiser
Carolyn Kell
Duane Kell
James Kelly-Rand
Sheila Kennedy
Edward Knowles
Rolando Kraeher
Michael Kramer
Catherine Kubic
Taruan Kumar
Chung Lun Kuo
Emily Kuo
Janet Kurtz
Brain Kwekel
Julie Lam
Robert Lang
Michael Lark
Gary Larsen
Matt LaRue
Milton Lau
Michael Lauber
Jessica Lavin
Chih-Ming Lee
Debbie Lee
Henry Leonardi
Andrea Letourneau
Pius Leuba
Chris Lewis
Dian Lim
Alison Liotta
James Lipscomb
Paul Logan
Catherine Logue
Christina Long
Elizabeth Long
Andrew Longmire
Barbara Lorenti
Avram Lothan
Kathy Lowney
Douglas Ludgin
Eric Lum
Linda Lyman
Joan MacKay- Smith
Hillary Maharam
Gulshan Malik
Alice Mande
Ronald Margolis
Richard Marshall
Crystal Martin
Stephanie Masher
Beth Masucci-Newman
Christine Mathew
Ross McCain
Michael McCann
Mollie McCardle

Michael McGroarty
Erinn McGurn
Jane McKinnell
Charlie McKinnery
David McLean
Patricia McManus
Julia McMorrough
Savanna McNeill
Sindu Meier
Marhea Melloh
Brian Mendelson
Oscar Mertz
Jim Michaels
Margaret Minor
Mary Mitchele
Michael Mlodgenski
Jessica Molinar
Steven Moon
Linvelle Morton
Christian Munoz
Sophia Nasto
Louise Nateshom
Farah Naz
Barton Nelson
Nancy Netzer
Marc Neveu
Elizabeth Newman
Trong Nguyen
Kayoko Ohtsuki
McDee Okafo
Christine O'Neil
Peter Osler
Mark Osterman
Mathew Oudens
Narin Oun
Kristin Palazola
Spiros Pantazi
Linda Papadopoulas
Irma Paronen
Stuart Parsons
Michael Pasquale
Paul Pasquariello
Paul Paukalis
John Paul
Lena Payne
Alex Peabody
Sandi Pederzini
Christiane Pein
Adolfo Pena-Iguaran
Alan Penney
Susan Personette
Frederick Petersen
Jill Peterson
Kristopher Pettersen
Gifford Pierce
Justin Pijak
Anthony Pisani
Holly Plumley
Kenneth Pollard
William Powell
Pamela Pratt
Mark Prendergast
Ligmie Preval
Christopher Pritchard
Penelope Prutsalis
Christopher Puzio
Gene Pyo
Timothy Quirk
Eric Reinhard
Kevin Renz
Timothy Rhoads
Edison Ribiero
Marie Ricci
Gerald Richert

Frederick Richter
Robert Rife
Kenneth Roberts
Susan Roberts
Thomas Robinson
Karen Roche
Elizabeth Roettger
Robert Rogers
Daniel Rothenberg
Edwin Rothfarb
Thomas Rourk
Paul Rovinelli
Laura Roy
Kristine Royal
Karen Ruan
Beth Rubenstein
Christine Rumi
Claudia Russell
Ali Sadr-Watson
Connie Saienga
John Salem
Jeff Salocks
Michael Schmitt
Matin Scholl
Rosemary Schrauth
Donna Schumacher
Andrew Scott
Clinton Scott
Christopher Scovel
Saara Seppanen Young
Michael Shagnon
Vera Shapiro
Robert Shearer
John Shelden
Young-Nae Shin
Stephen Siegle
Marshall Silva
Jose Silveira
John Simonetti
Nathaniel Skerry
Scott Slarsky
Nathaniel Slayton
Colin Smith
Donovan Smith
Gene Smith
Ivy Smith
Joan MacKay Smith
Tracy Smith
Vincent Snyder
Kavita Srinivasan
Michael Stanton
Martine Staublin
Bradley Stech
John Steffian
Sharon Steinberg
Eric Stern
Laura Stevens
Peter Stevens
Wade Stevens
John Stoddard
Alex Stolz
Judith Strayer
Gilbert Strickler
John Suarez
Jennifer Sullivan
Julie Sullivan
Sheila Sullivan
Heather Suranofsky
Carlena Suttles-Pate
Craig Sweeney
Joseph Szkolka
Emily Talcott
Eileen Tam
Cary Tamarkin

Aaron Taylor
Anna Marie Taylor
David Taylor
Donald Taylor
Timothy Techler
William Tecu
Todd Thiel
Scott Thomsen
Maggie Thomson
Sue Ann Thyng
Theodore Tickell
Ian Toeg
Julia Tombaugh
Susan Touloukian
Teresa Tourvas
Deirdre Townley
Anne Treloar
Kevin Triplett
David Tsai
Gordon Tully
Kristen Turnbull
Darlene Turner
Regina Vacaro
Jay Valenta
James Vaseff
Christine Verret
Kristina Vidal
Eric Viele
Ole Vijg
John Vinton
Robert Von Zumbusch
Kenneth Wade
Jeff Wagner
Nicholas Wagner
Roberta Wahl
Norman Wang
Carolyn Ward
Thomas Ward
Yoshiyuki Watanabe
Kurt Wehmann
James Weir
Susan Weller
Augustus Wendell
Jennifer Wennik
Andrew West
Kyung Mee Whang
Kenneth Whyte
Brooke Williams
David Williams
Elizabeth Williams
James Wilson
Mark Winford
Mary J. Wojewodzki
Michael Wolk
Brian Wong
Barry Wonnacott
Robert Wood
Jeffrey Wood
Charles Woods
Beth Worell
Weston Wright
Yling Wu
Magdaline Yeo
Mathieu Zahler
Erika Zekos
Barbara Zewiey
Ronald Zeytoonian
Xiaocun Zhu
Gregg Zurlow

# Photography Credits